How to Destroy a Village: What the Clintons Taught a Seventeen Year Old

By
Jason D. Fodeman

PublishAmerica
Baltimore

First printing

ISBN: 1-59129-804-0
PUBLISHED BY PUBLISHAMERICA BOOK
PUBLISHERS
www.publishamerica.com
Baltimore

Printed in the United States of America

DEDICATION

To my Uncle Robert and Bubbe Faye.
Wish you could be here to read my book,
but ultimately your good-natured attitudes helped
mold me into the young man I am today.

Thank you.

TABLE OF CONTENTS

FOREWORD

Ten years have passed since the Clintons and their Toadies undertook the infestation of the White House and the Executive Branch of Government. Throughout the next eight years the poison seeped into every branch of government, so that the political process itself was perhaps irrevocably damaged.

Throughout the Clinton administration, the American people were assaulted with a seemingly endless litany of scandals: Travelgate, Chinagate, Filegate, campaign finance abuses, perjury, obstruction of justice, witness tampering, and the like; all of which took the country and the Presidency to ever-descending levels of decadence and moral leprosy. Actions that, had they been committed twenty years earlier, would have resulted in mass demonstrations of outrage, were viewed with careless indifference by the electorate and members of the President's own party.

Where was the main-stream media during the eight-year saturnalia? The very ones upon whom the public placed its trust and confidence to report the truth without bias, were the most biased of all. So long as a Clintonian canard was spinnable, the media supinely reported the spin, so that the President was always portrayed as the victim of mean-spirited conspirators.

Nobody was immune from the vituperation and character assassination that emanated from the White House. Women who had been attacked, abused or harassed by Clinton, were portrayed as "trailer trash", bimbos", "money hungry predators" and worse. The attacks were ceaseless and unrelenting. Senators, Representatives, Judges and other officers of the court were likewise subjected to the spate of invective. And throughout it all, the "untrammelled" press swallowed whatever the spinmeisters fed them; and, in the interest of access and to further their own agenda, passed it on to the public as fact and truth. As a consequence of that almost universal misreporting and misconstruing of events, the public was denied information vital to a rational analysis of the President's conduct.

With the conscious and deliberate cooperation of the media,

President Clinton left office amid the obseqious plaudits of his followers. He had indeed fooled a great proportion of the public into believing that he had been a great president who had presided over "the most ethical presidency in history" - or so he thought.

When William Jefferson Clinton stood on the steps of the Capital, raised his right hand to God and swore to preserve, protect and defend the Constitution, Jason D. Fodeman, the author of this book, was only nine years old. His childhood, then, was contemporaneous with the Clinton era. Fortunately, Mr. Fodeman was raised in a functional family imbued with a strong moral sense. He tells us of the strong emphasis that his parents placed on honor, integrity, truth and respect for law. By the age of seventeen , those virtues were so ingrained in him as to be a part of his very being. He too was subjected to the eight-year spin cycle and one would think that his immature mind would have been skewed as had so many others. But that was not the case.

Immediately following the devastating vote to acquit Clinton in the Senate, I recall a conversation with Chairman Henry Hyde, of the House Judiciary Committee. I said, "You know, Mr. Hyde, it's bad enough that we just got clobbered in a rigged trial, but the American people hate our guts for even bringing the charges." Chairman Hyde smiled and said, "Dave, don't ever underestimate the decency and intelligence of the American people." Henry Hyde was right, and this book proves it. Despite the unremitting attempts to justify the President's conduct and to portray him as a loveable rogue, this young author was able to see through the smoke and mirrors and to discern the real situation.

All Americans should read this book, but especially those who proclaim that the Clinton years are behind us, and that we should move on because there are no lingering effects. This book gives the lie to any such statement. Mr. Fodeman, just a teenager, is able to identify the Clinton legacy more clearly than adults double or even triple his age. As is clear from a reading of this book, the Clinton gang represented a philosophy of win at any cost. Their motto is "the end justifies the means, and I will define the proper end." Mr.

Fodeman understands that such concepts are inimical to everything that he had been taught by his parents. Because of his upbringing, he is able to choose the right and separate truth from deception.

The daunting result of reading this book is that you will understand, perhaps for the first time, the devastating effect of the Clinton presidency on the moral structures of our society. But worse, you will view the entire sordid business from the aspect of a young adult. Mr. Fodeman was not drawn into the resulting moral anarchy, but how many of our children and grandchildren were? As the years pass will we encounter the amorality represented by the Clinton conduct in adults who were children during the nineties? Will that be the Clinton legacy? Let us all pray fervently that such will not be the case, and that Jason Fodeman represents our coming generation.

David P. Schippers

Part One
Introduction

Chapter 1
Myself

When Bill and Hillary Clinton entered the White House in January of 1993, most people either liked them or didn't. Just as most people either agreed with their beliefs or didn't. However, when Bill Clinton became president, I was only nine years old. I was a fourth grader at Long Lots Elementary School in Westport, Connecticut. I did not know anything about the Clintons personally or politically, which parallels the fact that I had no political beliefs at the time. My main concerns were playing Nintendo and learning how to do long division.

Eight quick years later, I transformed from a political know nothing to part of the evil "vast right-wing conspiracy" that is out to get the innocent Clintons. Obviously at age nine I was not against the Clintons, so something had to trigger or cause me to feel the way I do now.

The summer of 2000, I started getting interested in politics. I watched the news, mostly cable and some network. I read newspapers, books, and Internet articles. Facts I learned about the Clintons were so shocking and repulsive that it was hard for me to fathom how this family could rise to the most powerful office in our great country. It was these disturbing actions and the lessons the actions give that turned me against the Clintons.

It is a good thing I was brought up in such a moral household. My parents' strong emphasis on honor and integrity helped me avoid being sucked in by the Clintons' horrible examples. My parents taught me not to lie, to always obey the laws, and to treat others respectfully (even those I didn't like or agree with). The Clintons' actions were in direct conflict to all of these lessons. Even parental lessons that the Clintons' deeds in part corroborated, the Clintons still managed to put a corrupt, dishonest spin on them. Luckily my parents embedded so many principles in me that I was able to see the wrong in the Clintons' actions and was not seduced by the darker side. However, I fear that other teenagers who did not have as strong an upbringing as I did may have been negatively influenced by what the Clintons did. Many young adults are impressed by money and power. If they see a man who has both but has no integrity, these young adults may think inappropriate conduct is acceptable, even a justifiable means to an end.

Much attention has been given to the decline in youth values after events like the atrocious Columbine massacre. The experts and pundits often blame the easy-accessible R-rated movies that are filled with death, violence, sex, and profanity. Other experts reproach the rappers who produce CDs that glorify violence and profanity. Some denounce the excessively violent video games. The three above items may indeed be inappropriate and much too easily accessible to children. However, over those eight years the three were not nearly as prominent in our society as the former First Family.

The Clintons in a way were similar to these forms of entertainment in their effect on youth. No, the Clintons did not teach us violence, but the logic is the same: just as violent video games and rap music have some effect on children, so did the Clintons' behavior. Kids heard about the actions of the Clintons and just as with the video games, children have become desensitized to inappropriate actions while more impressionable children may have adopted the Clintons' modus operandi as their own. Kids learn from what they see and hear.

The Clintons' lessons may actually be worse. Rap, movies, and video games often exhibit negative aspects of violence. Movies may contain violence, but usually the bad guys don't get away scot free and aren't admired by millions of people. In most movies the villains are either killed or arrested showing kids the negative aspect of violence and the price that must be paid for such a lifestyle. The same can be said about violent video games too. If you keep playing, you will eventually lose or die.

Even vulgar rap music indirectly shows the negatives of the lifestyle mentioned in the music. The songs don't say violence is bad or not to do what the music says, but if you have followed the police reports lately you will be aware that rappers Jay-Z, Puff Daddy, DMX, and Eminem have all had problems with the law. Also in the past decade two rappers died in a way similar to their music.

Rap, movies, and video games indirectly show children that there will be dire consequences to their actions, but the same can not be said about the Clintons. The Clintons have demonstrated to kids do whatever you want and then cover up and do anything possible to evade responsibility. The Clintons did not really suffer from their behavior. The historic impeachment was treated more like a circus sideshow. They did not get into serious trouble and worst of all their methods prevailed in part because of a blind eye from the Justice Department and the media. However, the Justice Department will not look the other way for the average citizen. A young person who follows the Clinton formula will get no such free ride.

According to an analysis of Hillary Clinton's book, It Takes a Village, the book is titled after the African maxim, "'It takes a village to raise a child'" (Anderson, "It Takes a Village An Analysis of Hillary Clinton's Book"). I guess it all depends on what the definition of "village" is, but my definition is everyone in a community from salesmen to teachers to powerful politicians. That means that in the "village" of the United States the Clintons as the First Family had a key influence in the raising of each child. It was their role to set a moral and ethical example for the younger generation to learn from. As we all know, unfortunately they did not. In this book I show the clear negative lessons that the Clintons espoused. I have rejected their mantra and its likely consequences. Were you and your children able to?

I am a busy teenager who wrote this book to address the issue of the Clintons' influence on children that has thus far been ignored. Unlike catastrophic violence, children's everyday wrongdoing and its causes, which are much more rampant, have not been adequately explored. This book demonstrates how the Clintons lowered the bar for what is acceptable behavior in a civilized society.

Part Two
Lessons the Clintons Destroyed

Chapter 2
Laws Can Be Broken

One lesson my parents taught me was that wherever I go there will be laws and rules to follow. In my house, rules included getting my dad <u>The Wall Street Journal</u>, completing my homework, setting the dinner table, and bedtimes. These rules applied only to me. At school there were more rules such as no fighting, no disruptive behavior, and no inappropriate language. These rules affected every student at the schools I attended. Not only does each institution and domicile have its own set of rules, but the government also establishes laws. My parents said that although some rules and laws may seem unfair they are for the good of the people and the country. If I did not follow the laws of the land, I would plain and simply be caught and punished. Not only could violating criminal laws ruin my life, but it is also imperative that each individual follows the rule of the land for our great country to grow and prosper.

A great threat to my law-abiding ways were Bill and Hillary Clinton. Both have allegedly broken laws and gotten away with their wrongdoings. The Clintons have committed improper, possibly illegal behavior, and have been involved with more questionable activity in order not to get caught. Prior malfeasance spawned new scandalous activity. These alleged initial infractions include assaulting Juanita Broaddrick, the groping of Kathleen Willey, Castle Grande, TravelGate, campaign finance violations, and ChinaGate. These events led to a full-fledged effort of cover ups because the Clintons do not care about our laws, they care about not getting caught.

Juanita Broaddrick

One of Bill Clinton's flaws is his propensity for illicit affairs. Cheating on one's wife does not set the best example for young people, but it does not break any laws. However, rape does.

Juanita Broaddrick is a nurse who claimed that Bill Clinton raped her in 1978 when he was the Attorney General of Arkansas. She is a successful, accomplished woman who wanted no money or civil damages. Her story is also confirmed by four witnesses who had nothing to gain by supporting her, but lots to lose (Rabinowitz, "Wall Street Journal Editorial Commentary-Juanita Broaddrick Meets the Press). For many years, Juanita Broaddrick refused to publicly reveal her story, fearing no one would believe it. She reluctantly came forward after becoming annoyed with rampant rumors on the Internet. The tabloid, <u>Star</u>, angered her further when it alleged the Clintons bought her silence, "'It was so hurtful, to think anyone would think we would take money'" (Barringer, "On Tortuous Route, Sexual Assault Accusation Against Clinton Resurfaces"). Broaddrick is no Webster Hubbell. She sought no money and only came forward to clear her name, giving her story credibility.

Broaddrick's story is that in 1978 she was working at a nursing home where Attorney General Clinton, who was running for governor, made a campaign stop. Clinton invited Broaddrick to visit his campaign headquarters in Little Rock. The next week Broaddrick went to Little Rock for a seminar of the American College of Nursing Home Administrators. She called campaign headquarters and was connected to Clinton at his apartment. The two arranged to meet in the coffee shop of the Camelot Hotel, but went up to Broaddrick's room because it was too noisy. According to Broaddrick, after five minutes of being in the room, Clinton put his arm around her. He then said that they were both married people. To show her lack of interest in him, Broaddrick said that she was also involved with another man, her future husband. Clinton's lust was not deterred. He then allegedly got her on the bed, held her down, bit her lip, and raped her. Broaddrick said "'I felt paralyzed and was starting to cry'" (Rabinowitz, "Wall Street Journal Editorial Commentary-Juanita Broaddrick Meets the Press).

Broaddrick's friend, Norma Rogers, who accompanied Broaddrick on the trip, found her on the bed in a state of shock. The two then drove home discussing how a man like Bill Clinton could become governor (Rabinowitz, "Wall Street Journal Editorial Commentary-Juanita Broaddrick Meets the Press).

The Juanita Broaddrick allegations are indeed disturbing. The Juanita Broaddrick scandal is different from other scandals about the Clintons. It was the best chance to hold Clinton accountable for his actions. By the time Clinton was governor and president, along with some biased media assistance, he had the power and connections to provide a degree of protection for himself in the various scandals. However, as attorney general, if the allegation had arisen, he might have had to deal with the claim. Although Broaddrick was afraid no one would believe her at the time, had she come forward, she might have been able to get justice.

I realize that the rape charge along with most Clinton scandals are just "allegations." Usually when several people level similar claims, a serious effort can be expected to proceed to the next level via arrest and prosecution. In the normal circumstances the claim of one woman is sufficient and can adversely effect the reputation of the accused even if the accusation is proven false. As we will learn with Clinton, numerous sexual harassment claims were not enough to even draw the ire of Patricia Ireland and her ilk.

Kathleen Willey

The rape claim of Juanita Broaddrick is one of many allegations regarding President Clinton's physical abuses of women. Kathleen Willey claimed that Clinton forcibly groped her. Similar to Broaddrick, Willey is a credible witness. She has made a couple of mistakes in her past, as exemplified by a high school pregnancy, but regardless, up until the incident she was a loyal Democrat and a friend of Bill Clinton. Willey assisted numerous Democratic campaigns, including Chuck Robb and Governor Douglas Wilder. In 1989 Willey met Governor Clinton at a Charlottesville fund-raiser. After a 1992 debate in Richmond, she ecstatically introduced him to other distinguished Democrats (Bellafante, "The Lives of Kathleen Willey"). Kathleen Willey was surely not out to get her Democratic friend, so her story has credibility.

Kathleen Willey claimed that on November 29, 1993 she went to the White House to ask President Clinton for a government job. Willey says that in a hallway off the Oval Office, Clinton gave her a big hug. This was usual for Willey because Clinton always gave Willey big hugs when he saw her. But Clinton gave Willey another slightly longer hug and kissed her on the mouth. Willey was surprised and pulled away, but as she did, he touched her breasts with his hand. Then Clinton shook her hand and put it on his aroused genitals. Willey left the office in disbelief of Clinton's reckless behavior ("Excerpt from Kathleen Willey's Interview with 60 minutes").

What Willey described is a forced, unwanted sexual advance, as NOW and other feminist groups usually would be quick to point out, but not this time. Forced unwanted, sexual advances can cause serious emotional problems and should not be committed by anyone, especially not by the President of the United States. So the issue is, did Willey tell the truth? I believe the answer is yes because Willey was granted a meeting with President Clinton in the White House. Very few citizens are given this prestigious opportunity. The simple fact that Willey was in a position to meet with the president in the Oval Office gives her credibility.

If the allegation is true, why hasn't Bill Clinton been punished? The reason is simple with respect to Kathleen Willey, Bill Clinton did not just abuse her, he did all he could to discredit her.

Castle Grande

As we know, there was a myriad of other scandals involving the Clintons that were not just about sex. One of these was a land deal called Castle Grande in which both Clintons were involved.

James McDougal, the Clinton's Whitewater partner and the owner of Madison Guaranty Savings & Loan, adeptly turned large plots of rural land into residential projects. McDougal desired to do this with the 1,000 acre Castle Grande land, hoping to create half-acre lots into homesites for working class families. The land was priced at $1.75 million, but McDougal could only borrow $600,000 from his own bank. Seth Ward, McDougal's friend, agreed to pay the remaining $1.15 million. Ward borrowed the money from Madison Guaranty in a "non-recourse" loan. Ward did not have to repay it because if the reason for the loan were known, McDougal would have been in serious trouble. After McDougal extended the loan to Ward, he made other transactions to cover it up (Young, "The Castle Grande Deal").

David Hale, a municipal judge who ran Capital Management Services, Inc., abetted the cover up. His company made loans to minorities and the economically disadvantaged, which the Small Business Administration matched and backed. Hale, McDougal, and Jim Guy Tucker, Clinton's Lieutenant Governor, connived to use Hale's company to generate additional loans for Madison. The plan was purposefully confusing in order to fool the authorities. A convoluted set of transactions ensued essentially concealing that the property was purchased entirely with Madison money, clearing Madison from Ward's loan, and producing commissions for Madison (Young, "The Castle Grande Deal").

Hillary Clinton played a pivotal role in the scandal. Mrs. Clinton produced an option agreement that gave Seth Ward $300,000 in commissions when he sold his Castle Grande holdings. The agreement further cloaked the Castle Grande corruption ("Rose law firm billing records").

President Clinton was also allegedly involved in the scandal. According to Hale and confirmed by Trooper L.D. Brown, before Christmas of 1985, Governor Clinton went up to Hale on the steps of the Capitol Building and said, "'Are you going to help Jim and me out?'" ("Evidence in Whitewater Case is Now Firm").

Before the Castle Grande loans were made, Hale testified that McDougal, Clinton, and Hale met at the Castle Grande Office to discuss a fraudulent loan from Hale's company to Susan McDougal ("David Hale's Testimony"). Hale accused President Clinton of pressuring him to make the loan. At first James McDougal rejected Hale's claim, but supported it before he died. McDougal said that Clinton attended the meeting with Hale and asked Hale for help with the loan (Franken, "McDougal Changing Tune on Clinton-Hale meeting").

So if Hillary Clinton was involved in the creation of a document to deceive regulators and Bill Clinton was involved with an illegal loan, how come they were not punished and how on earth was Bill Clinton able to get any job, let alone become president with this major skeleton in his closet? The reason is simple. Did Bill and Hillary Clinton just once accidentally break the law and then play by the rules? The answer is no. Once the Clintons did these two questionable things, they allegedly did everything within their means to see that the truth was delayed and never found, so they could escape blame and punishment.

TravelGate

Another scandal involving the Clinton administration was the firing of seven innocent career Travel Office workers, including the persecution of the director, Billy Dale. It all started during the Clinton transition when the President's cousin, Catherine Cornelius, joined forces with the travel company, World Wide Travel, to support the changing of White House travel operations. Also during the transition, Harry Thomason, the owner of the air charter company that serviced the Clinton/Gore campaign, met with Hillary Clinton and suggested that the Travel Office employees be removed because of their lack of loyalty ("Investigation of the White House Travel Firings and Related Matters").

Thomason started disseminating rumors of wrongdoing to the Clintons. On April 16, 1993, Thomason contacted David Watkins, White House Director of Administration, and alleged that the Travel Office workers were taking five percent kickbacks. In May of 1993 there were numerous conversations between Thomason and both Clintons. On May 14, 1993, after a dinner with Thomason, Mrs. Clinton sent a message to Watkins saying "'we need to get those people out' and 'our people in'" ("Investigation of the White House Travel Firings and Related Matters").

In a May 16, 1993 meeting between Mrs. Clinton and Chief of Staff Mack McLarty, Mrs. Clinton pressured McLarty to fire the Travel Office workers. The next day McLarty went to Watkins and said that the travel office affair was very important to Mrs. Clinton. In a memo, Watkins wrote that he knew there "'would be hell to pay'" if he did not comply with the First Lady's desires. On this day President Clinton was briefed about the upcoming firings and on May 19, 1993, the Travel Office Workers were fired ("Investigation of the White House Travel Firings and Related Matters").

Although firing long-time government employees to make room for campaign contributors is not the most honorable action, it is not illegal. However, the Clinton White House did not want bad press, so they based the firing on biased, groundless allegations. To show that the allegations were serious, a thirty month investigation ensued into former Travel Office Director Billy Dale (Clinger, "Statement on the White House Travel Office"). In the investigation the Department of Justice failed to discover any evidence pertaining to Dale and no witnesses provided information against Dale. Regardless, the government accused Dale of stealing $68,000. The prosecution's argument was farcical. They said he stole to enable his wife to go to a hairdresser and to buy large quantities of groceries for the Dale's vacation home. There was scant evidence for a case, but one proceeded. When it ended, the jury acquitted Dale after only two hours of deliberation ("Investigation of the White House Travel Firings and Related Matters"). The innocent Dale was finally free from the Clinton administration's political harassment; however, he owed $500,000 in legal fees (Clinger, "Statement on the White House Travel Office").

It seems the Clinton White House abused its power to instigate the prosecution against Dale, which is probably illegal. There was no reason for a trial, but the White House used its clout for purely political reasons.

In essence TravelGate is similar to the Castle Grande scandal. The Clintons played a big part in the Travel Office firings. Once the firings occurred and proved unpopular, however, the Clintons did everything in their power to conceal their involvement.

Campaign Finance Abuses

Finding there was no need for ethics in the White House, the Clinton/ Gore administration devised an unethical, possibly illegal plan to raise money. The scheme consisted of using federal property to sell access. The Clinton team raised money for the 1996 reelection bid and for Hillary Clinton's senatorial bid.

It is known that Bill Clinton and his administration misused federal property as early as 1994. Harold Ickes, former White House aide, testified that in 1994 Bill Clinton called Democratic donors from the White House to seek contributions. Administration officials did not dispute Ickes statement (The Associates Press, "Ickes reportedly told of Clinton calls from White House").

The fact that Ickes is a trusted, Clinton advisor and that the administration officials did not refute the charges indicates the odds are the accusation is true. This means President Clinton may have broken a law. Federal law forbids government officials from soliciting campaign donations from a federal building or on federal property. It does not matter whether President Clinton called a couple of times or thousands of times, either way he should have been investigated and held responsible like most people who get caught breaking a law. As you and I know, he was not punished and the fundraising on government property never stopped.

In 1994 while Clinton made those phone calls to solicit funds, he was also hosting private breakfasts with affluent Democrats to raise money for the party's health care program. In a May 9, 1994 memo, Ickes wrote that "'BC will have breakfast – to raise $'" (The Associated Press, "Clinton had fundraising breakfasts in '94"). The White House admitted that Bill or Hillary Clinton hosted at least ten breakfasts or lunches at the executive mansion. An anonymous person familiar with the breakfasts stated that they were orchestrated to yield funds. Attendees may not have been specifically solicited at the breakfasts, but knew the administration and the Democratic Party expected money. Some attendees gave generous five and six figure donations soon after their visits (The Associated Press, "Clinton had fundraising breakfasts in '94").

The above breakfasts are similar to the phone calls in that both involved the use of federal property to raise money. However, the 1994 White House fundraising was nothing compared to that of 1995 and 1996.

In 1995, President Clinton authorized using the White House to solicit and reward big donors. The perks included jogs with the president, White House coffees, and overnights in the Lincoln bedroom. The idea of the Lincoln bedroom specifically came up in a January 5, 1995 memo from Terry McAuliffe, then National Finance Chairman of the DNC, as a way to get money. Clinton liked the idea, writing, "'Ready to start overnights right away'" (Baker, "President had Big Role in Setting Donor Perks"). In the memo, McAuliffe included the names of the top ten supporters, but Clinton suggested that McAuliffe also solicit people who had given and would give $50,000 and $100,000 (Baker, "President had Big Role in Setting Donor Perks").

In 1995 and 1996 Lincoln bedroom guests gave at least $5.2

million to the DNC. The biggest donors were investor Dirk Ziff who gave $411,000 and movie producer Steven Spielberg who gave $336,000. Twenty-four overnight guests gave at least $100,000 to the DNC ("Lincoln Bedroom Guests Gave DNC At Least $5.2 Million"). So much money for just a one night stay, they should have at least held out for the administration's going out of business pardon sale!

The Clinton administration used the Lincoln bedroom of the White House to raise millions of dollars although the law states federal property can not be used to raise money. President Clinton should be accountable because not only is it his administration, but apparently he authorized the usage.

Before the 1996 election the Clinton White House also hosted coffees to raise money. The coffees were a fundraising event that rewarded major donors with access. Between January 11, 1995 and August 23, 1996 there were 103 of these coffees, of which the president attended the majority. The coffee guests gave a total of $26.4 million or $54,000 per guest for the 1996 election. DNC documents refer to the coffees as political fundraisers. For example, a memoranda Ickes prepared for the President and the Vice President classified them as "'political/fundraising coffees'" ("Majority Report: Executive Summary").

The coffees were treated just like any other fundraiser. Ickes would regularly inform President Clinton and Vice President Gore about the projected and actual amount donated. Furthermore, two anonymous DNC officials said the Party's Finance Chairman Marvin Rosen informed supporters that $50,000 would buy coffee with President Clinton (LaFraniere, "Clinton Told of Cash Raised From Coffees).

In similar fashion Al Gore utilized the White House to solicit money via phone calls. He made approximately forty-five calls from his White House Office, raising around $800,000 for the DNC, of which $100,000 was "hard money" (Majority Report: Executive Summary).

The First Lady was also allegedly involved. White House

workers were concerned that she used the Lincoln Bedroom to attract and reward contributors. At least twenty-six couples stayed overnight in the Lincoln Bedroom after donating or promising to donate to her campaign (Cosby, "Sources: Mrs. Clinton Gave Lincoln Bedroom to Big Donors").

The Clintons transformed the White House into Sotheby's. Everything was up for sale to the highest bidder. Yet, nothing was ever done about the evidence indicating the misuse of federal property. Bill Clinton was never forced to resign or kicked out of office for breaking campaign finance laws. There wasn't even a slap on the wrist. Ideally people go to jail when they get caught breaking laws, but for the Clintons it was just another day at 1600 Pennsylvania Avenue. As usual the Clintons denied their role, and their appointed friends in the Justice Department made sure that justice was not carried out.

ChinaGate

Unfortunately, fundraising from federal property was just the tip of the iceberg. I am referring to the large amount of money that came to the Clintons from overseas. Coincidentally during Clinton's terms our country lost some of its nuclear secrets. Some believe that President Clinton is the reason.

The Lippo Group is an Indonesian conglomerate run by Mochtar Riady and his son, James Riady. There has been a longstanding relationship between the Riady family and President Clinton that began when he was Governor of Arkansas. In 1984 along with financier Jack Stephens, the Riady family bought a bank in Little Rock, Arkansas. James Riady was sent to Little Rock to assist bank operations. It was there that James Riady met Clinton at one of Stephens' weekly lunches ("Campaign Finance Key Players: The Riady Family").

In China Lippo has a partnership with China Resources Holding Co. According to Defense Intelligence Agency (DIA) analyst Nicholas Eftimiades and investigator Thomas R. Hampson, the company is used for spying ("U.S. National Security and Military/ Commercial Concerns with the People's Republic of China").

The Lippo Group and its subsidiaries gave President Clinton key financial support throughout his career. In 1992 the Riadys loaned Clinton $3 million, saving Clinton's presidential campaign. Other assistance came from, John Huang, a top Lippo executive, who secured a $250,000 contribution to the DNC. The Wiriadinata family, which was connected to Lippo, donated $425,000 to the DNC. Many other people and companies with ties to the Lippo Group donated substantial amounts of money to the Clintons and to Democrats ("Lippo Scandal Unfolds The White House Indonesia Connection").

Why did the Lippo Group give all this money? One logical answer is that they wanted to purchase influence and gain knowledge. Allegedly this knowledge was acquired through top Lippo executive, John Huang. On January 31, 1994, Huang received a top secret security clearance. The normal background investigation was bypassed. The Office of Personal Management checked his background instead of the FBI, so suspicious overseas connections were not looked into. At this time Huang had top secret clearance and was an executive of a company with ties to Chinese intelligence (Coulter 247).

In the summer of 1994, John Huang was given a job at the Commerce Department as Deputy Assistant Secretary for International Economic Policy. Sources have stated that the Riadys vaunted that they bought his position. At Commerce, Huang accessed numerous intelligence material and frequently called Lippo after viewing this material (Coulter 246).

In review, Clinton's friend with connections to Chinese Intelligence, James Riady, gave Clinton and Democrats money. An executive of Riady's Lippo Group was given top secret clearance and made numerous calls to Lippo after seeing top secret documents. Chinese intelligence could have accessed all the information that was relayed back. It thus seems to me that President Clinton's associations may have played a role in the breach of security that occurred on his watch. If this assumption is true, why was Clinton allowed to finish two presidential terms and why was his wife able to become "'pres'"? Oops, I mean "'a first-term senator'" from New York ("Hillary's presidential Slip Showing"). The answer is that the Clintons did all they could to hide their Chinese connections to avoid scrutiny.

Summary

The scandals mentioned in this chapter all involve President Clinton directly or indirectly because he is responsible for the actions of his administration. A couple of the scandals involved Hillary Clinton. All were unethical and some probably illegal, but somehow President Clinton was never held accountable. Although many Clinton aides, friends, and associates were punished for their involvement, the Clintons have always been able to evade responsibility.

The original scandals, which are talked about in this chapter are well known, but much less known are the sleazy tactics the Clintons used to see that they remained just minor bumps in the road of their political ambitions as opposed to an unsurpassable gorge.

What one learns from these scandals is what matters most is getting where you want and staying there. What you do to reach the goal is insignificant. Be as Machiavellian as you want. Do what you have to do and what you want to do. Just don't get caught and make sure you are not held responsible for your actions.

This poses a major problem for children and our country. During the Clinton administration it seemed that almost everyday a new scandal emerged surrounding the Clintons. When children and adults constantly hear about the First Family, which should serve as a positive role model, immersed in scandals, people begin to get desensitized by illegal and immoral behavior. They think, well, if the President of the United States can do it, so can I. They hear so much about wrong behavior they are brainwashed into thinking that it is acceptable and the norm.

This raises serious problems for our country and for many people. If people feel illegal and immoral actions are acceptable, they will think they can behave in similar fashion. The difference is the Clintons in the White House had tremendous power behind them. They also had ninety-three United States Attorneys, an Attorney General, and a FBI Director, all of whom President Clinton (probably in conjunction with his wife) had appointed. The Clintons had the power and connections to see that they were not held accountable. Most people do not have that power. If we do inappropriate things, we will be caught, punished, and maybe even thrown in jail. Odds are no one will contribute to our legal defense funds either.

Chapter 3
Don't Take Responsibility

Another lesson my parents taught me is that everyone makes mistakes and occasionally will get into a bad situation. When this happens they said you must not try to cover up your wrongdoing because eventually the truth will prevail. If you tried to hide your involvement, you will just get into more trouble. For example, as a child while taking a cookie from the cookie jar, I accidentally bumped the jar causing it to fall on the floor and shatter into pieces. My parents raised me to take responsibility for my actions. They told me not to hide the pieces, hope no one noticed, and if someone did, play dumb and blame the dog. According to my parents, that was wrong and in the end they would find out the truth. Obfuscation would result in more problems for me and also taking responsibility is the best way I could learn from my mistakes.

It seems the lesson of taking responsibility is an unknown rule in the lives of the Clintons. They have been involved in more inappropriate behavior to see that their roles in the previous scandals were not discovered and that they were never held accountable. The Clintons have possibly been involved in obstruction of justice and witness tampering to prevent the demise of their political careers. Besides the Clintons' misdeeds and their efforts to conceal them, the worst part is that the cover up worked. Contrary to my parents' advice, the Clintons were able to thwart investigators, delay investigations, and to my surprise complete two terms in the White House.

Hillary Clinton's Billing Records

Hillary Clinton's mysterious, disappearing billing records conveniently delayed scrutiny and concealed her work with Madison Guaranty, specifically on the Castle Grande project.

In 1992 when questions about Whitewater first arose, Vince Foster and Webster Hubbell, two Rose Law Firm partners of Hillary Clinton and close friends of the Clinton family, removed the copy of her billing records. In early 1994, Independent Counsel Robert Fiske subpoenaed those records and in October of 1995 so did the Senate Whitewater Committee. The files disappeared into oblivion and were not turned over. Hubbell testified that he saw them during the 1992 campaign in the possession of Vince Foster, but authorities could not question Foster, who had died. While Hillary Clinton stated through her attorney that she "'may have'" reviewed them during the campaign but lacked knowledge of their current location (Zeifman, "Zeifman Memo to Rep. Barr on Clinton Impeachment").

In August 1995 a presidential aide, Carolyn Huber, discovered the missing billing records in the book room of the White House residence, adjacent to Mrs. Clinton's office. Mrs. Clinton was clueless as to how the documents got there, but only the Clintons and a few friends had access to the room. Huber testified that she did not realize that they were the billing records until five months later while sorting documents. Two years after the initial subpoena the authorities finally received them (Zeifman, "Zeifman Memo to Rep. Barr on Clinton Impeachment").

The billing records indicated Mrs. Clinton worked sixty hours for Madison over a fifteen month period. She met with and called Seth

Ward, a key player in Castle Grande deal, over a dozen times. She also produced an option apparently intended to befuddle investigators that provided $300,000 in commissions on the resale of his Castle Grande holdings. The records also indicated an April 7, 1986 phone call between Mrs. Clinton and the then Madison loan officer, Don Denton. He recalled that Mrs. Clinton realized the sleazy intention of the transaction. The billing records also have questions in Foster's handwriting most likely directed to Mrs. Clinton. Her fingerprints are also on the documents ("Rose law firm billing records").

The records brought intriguing information to the fore. They made public Mrs. Clinton's involvement in the Castle Grande deal. Bill and Hillary Clinton were the only people who benefited from the records' disappearance, and the only ones with a motive to keep them hidden.

The reappearance of the records in the book room of the White House residence cast further suspicion on the Clintons. This room was only accessible to the Clintons and specific friends, so it is hard to fathom how the documents just randomly wound up there without the Clintons knowing. If the Feds find drugs in a person's house with his fingerprints all over the contraband, that person will be charged, probably convicted and sentenced. What the Clintons had in their impenetrable, highly secured abode was analogous to finding drugs. They had subpoenaed documents. Knowing the whereabouts of subpoenaed documents and withholding constitutes obstruction of justice. But unlike the man with drugs in his house, the Clintons never stood trial and never went to jail.

Vince Foster's Office

Vince Foster was a friend of the Clintons in Arkansas who became a top aide in the Clinton White House. On July 20, 1993, Vince Foster was found dead in Fort Marcy Park in Virginia. The death of Vince Foster was a tragedy. Not just because a man met an untimely demise, but also because the authorities were unable to secure Foster's office. This mishap resulted in the removal and disappearance of important documents pertaining to Whitewater and TravelGate.

Foster was a key player in the firing of the Travel Office staff and the cover up. Foster attended a meeting with Harry Thomason, Catherine Cornelius, and David Watkins regarding the firing of the workers. Foster delegated his former law partner, William Kennedy to look into financial improprieties at the office. Kennedy wrote that "'Once this made it on the First Lady's agenda, Vince Foster became involved, and he and Harry Thomason regularly informed me of her attention to the Travel Office situation--as well as her insistence that the situation be resolved immediately by replacing the Travel Office Staff'" ("The Special Committee's Whitewater Report"). Foster was a conduit, communicating the First Lady's desire for the firing and is believed kept records in his office ("The Special Committee's Whitewater Report").

Foster also had a major involvement in Whitewater, crafting the sale of the Clintons' Whitewater share to the McDougals. His White House job involved incorporating the sale of the Clintons' Whitewater land into their 1992 tax returns. Thus, controversial and quite possibly incriminating Whitewater documents were suspected housed in Foster's office when he died ("The Special Committee's Whitewater Report"). Some believe that Hillary Clinton's billing records were also in his office at that time.

When Foster died, the Clintons could have let the normal search of a crime scene take place, but this might have had devastating effects. The Clintons wanted the public to know as little as possible about Whitewater and TravelGate. The Clintons did not want to be kicked out of office and certainly did not want to go from the White House to the "big house." The only way to keep the truth about those two scandals and possibly others hidden was to prevent the authorities from perusing the documents. The events that followed, at the least, smelled like an attempt to hinder the investigation.

On the evening of July 20, 1993, nine different law enforcement officials remembered four requests to secure Foster's office. Park

Police investigator, Sergeant Cheryl Braun, asked David Watkins to seal the office. Detective John Rolla confirmed this testimony. Rather than comply with the request, Watkins paged his assistant, Patsy Thomasson, and asked her to search the office. Counsel to the President, Bernard Nussbaum, accompanied Thomasson on the search. Margaret Williams, the First Lady's Chief of Staff, also searched the office that night. Instead of having the office secured, loyal, top Clinton aides performed an improper search of the office ("The Special Committee's Whitewater Report").

It is unknown who ordered Ms. Williams to search the office, but it is known that at 10:13 p.m. the Rodham residence called her. At 12:15 a.m. she was paged by Susan Thomases, a top Hillary Clinton aide, who the Rodham residence contacted about an hour before. Then at 12:56 a.m. Williams called the Rodham residence and at 1:10 a.m. she contacted Thomases. The order of the calls leads me to believe that Williams called Thomases and the First Lady to report on the search ("The Special Committee's Whitewater Report").

Not only did Williams enter a crime scene that should have been sequestered, but a credible witness with no reason to lie testified she removed files from Foster's office. Secret Service Officer Harry O'Neill swore under oath that on the night of Foster's death after being introduced to Williams by her assistant, Evelyn Lieberman, he saw Williams take file folders, three to five inches thick, from the office ("The Special Committee's Whitewater Report"). Why would Margaret Williams have a desire to search the office and why would she want to remove documents possibly pertaining to Hillary Clinton's scandals? A logical explanation is that Williams' boss ordered her to do so.

On the day after the death, Nussbaum made an agreement with Justice Department officials to allow the authorities to jointly examine documents in the office. The next day Williams called the Rodham residence at 7:44 a.m. The Rodham residence then called at 7:57 a.m. Susan Thomases who paged Nussbaum at 8:01 a.m. When Nussbaum returned the page, he testified that Thomases said, "'people are concerned'" about the arrangements that would have allowed law enforcement officials to review documents. ("The Special Committee's Whitewater Report"). Later that day Nussbaum changed his mind and decided not to give law enforcement officials such power. It seems quite obvious that those early morning calls changed Nussbaum's mind ("The Special Committee's Whitewater Report").

The modified procedure involved Nussbaum reviewing the documents in front of law officers and giving vague descriptions about the documents. He did not inform the people present about the files pertaining to Whitewater. Neither did he inform them about the notebook in Foster's briefcase regarding the Travel Office firings. Nussbaum took this notebook and kept it in his office until March 1994 when he resigned. After the worthless review was completed before the law officers, Nussbaum and Williams did the real examination. Williams took the Clintons' personal files from the office and brought them to the residence. Williams told Thomas Castleton that "'the President or the First Lady had to review the contents of the boxes to determine what was in them'" ("The Special Committee's Whitewater Report").

Deborah Gorham, Foster's secretary, confirmed that documents pertaining to the Clintons were removed. She kept indexes for all of his files, but on July 22, 1993 she noticed the one that listed the Clintons' personal documents was missing ("The Special Committee's Whitewater Report"). Logically the index would be missing because this would prevent investigators from knowing the specific documents taken.

The pattern of telephone calls and her top aide's involvement give credence that Mrs. Clinton masterminded the removal of documents. Removing the documents did not benefit Margaret Williams, but she did have much to lose because she could have been prosecuted. Hillary Clinton had everything to gain because in July of 1993 the public did not know everything it knows now about the Clinton's modus operandi. If the law enforcement officers had seen the documents, they might have learned more about the Clintons' involvement in Whitewater, TravelGate, and who knows what else.

The release of this information all at once would have been very damaging to the administration, so Hillary Clinton had to prevent scrutiny of the documents. The best way to do this was to have them removed from the scene. Therefore, to see that the Clintons' past involvement in scandals was not known, Hillary Clinton had to become involved in a plot to delay the authorities' access to the documents, which was very possibly illegal. However, Hillary Clinton and Margaret Williams never went to trial and were never convicted.

EmailGate

In the Clinton White House, controversial documents that shed light on Clinton scandals were not the only things that opportunely disappeared. Many emails were not properly archived and were thus lost.

In 1998 it was realized that the White House's Automated Records Management System (ARMS) email system was not working properly. Accounts were coded incorrectly, causing the system not to store emails. The specific number of emails not archived properly is unknown, but probably was between 100,000 and 250,000 emails. The email problem, which lasted from August 1996 to November 1998, affected the emails of about 500 top White House aides including President Clinton and the First Lady ("You've Lost Mail: The White House Email Saga").

The law states the White House must archive all emails so the White House Counsel can review and turn them over in response to subpoenas (Safire, "The 100,000 E-Mail Gap"). The missing emails were significant because they allegedly contained information about such Clinton scandals as Clinton/Gore campaign finance abuses, ChinaGate, the Monica Lewinsky scandal, and FileGate. These emails were subpoenaed but authorities never received them (Anderson, "Burton Calls for Special Counsel on Missing White House Email").

Sheryl Hall, a career federal government employee claimed that

Hillary Clinton's office plotted to hide emails from investigators (Sperry, "CNN, ABC spike reports after taping interviews with e-mail whistle-blower").

Unfortunately, there was never a real investigation into EmailGate, so no concrete evidence exists against the Clintons. However, one must take note that for such smart people with highly talented aides, the Clinton administration had a lot of computer glitches, destroyed hard drives, "bureaucratic snafu," and disappearing documents, which all have coincidentally been rather advantageous to the Clintons. The missing emails were no different. If the White House stored the emails properly, investigators would have been given new knowledge and possibly a smoking gun to some scandal. There was a motive for the Clintons to have the emails misplaced. As a concerned citizen who believes that character and integrity should be mandatory for high-ranking politicians, I hope the emails are retrieved and scrutinized before the 2004 presidential election, especially if Hillary Clinton is a candidate.

Like all Clinton scandals, it seems the White House orchestrated a full-fledged effort to conceal the email problem and the Justice Department ignored it.

TrooperGate

The Clintons' desire to have their indecorous actions suppressed went well beyond disappearing documents and emails. Numerous allegations existed involving Bill Clinton in plots to keep witnesses quiet or change their story.

According to specific Arkansas State troopers, Governor Clinton used them to help him cheat on his wife. Their duties included driving Clinton to meeting points, securing these points, bringing presents to women, watching Hillary, and lying to her about her husband's activities (Brock, "Living With the Clintons Bill's Arkansas bodyguards tell the story the press missed"). The troopers also claim to have witnessed other scandals such as Clinton's role in an illegal Hale loan. This disturbing information could have cost

Clinton his political career and definitely the 1992 election.

It seems that Clinton knew this, thus he tried to compel the troopers into never telling and recanting their stories once they did. Regardless, four troopers were interviewed by David Brock from late August to October of 1993. Two of the troopers, Larry Patterson and Roger Perry, agreed to go on the record while the other two did not. According to Perry, Trooper Danny Ferguson, one of the troopers that did not go on the record, told Perry that while on duty Governor Clinton contacted him at least twice. In the first call, Clinton instructed Ferguson to tell Perry that silence would be rewarded. Furthermore, Perry alleged that Clinton offered Ferguson a federal job if he remained mute. If true, this would violate the law. Soliciting anything of value in exchange for the promise of federal employment is illegal (Brock, "Living With the Clintons Bill's Arkansas bodyguards tell the story the press missed").

As with all Clinton allegations, the question is did it happen. In light of David Brock's subsequent conversion to liberalism and recantation of many statements, his musings must be carefully evaluated. Yet considerable corroboration exists and where there is so much smoke, often it is reasonable to believe there is fire. We know Clinton has a propensity not to admit or recall specific scandal details, which taints his credibility. Maybe Perry lied. However, I do not believe Perry was so naïve to fabricate about Clinton. Perry was constantly around Clinton. He must have witnessed Clinton's attack team adamantly pursuing accusers and informers. Clinton had a motive to attempt to buy Ferguson's cooperation and lie about it. The information Ferguson and the troopers allegedly knew could have damaged Clinton politically at the very least. If Clinton would lie to the public about Lewinsky in order to keep his job, surely he would be willing to do it in 1993.

The TrooperGate cover up involved Trooper L.D. Brown as well. He worked in Clinton's security detail from 1982 to 1985. Brown claimed that while riding on a public bus near Leicester, England on June 16, 1997 at 2 a.m., a man familiar with Brown's situation approached him. The man endeavored to influence Brown's upcoming testimony by offering him $100,000 and a job. Brown was told the job would be initiated through someone in the National Security Council. According to Brown, the man made a second offer over the telephone. Brown also said that in 1994 Skip Rutherford, a state Democratic Party official and a Clinton advocate, visited Brown urging him not to cooperate with Whitewater investigators ("The Washington Times-Ex-Trooper Will Tell of Bribery Attempt").

Attempting to influence Brown's testimony would comprise illegal witness tampering. Although no smoking gun, is it possible that President Clinton was involved in the plot? Was there a plot at all? Is any of it true? It is another "he said she said" situation. What we do know for sure is Clinton's history of doing anything and saying anything to get out of a tough situation. Furthermore, Clinton had no way of knowing at the time how much the public was prepared to accept. In retrospect, he certainly would not have lost any sleep over these allegations. The public loved him and the evidence be damned.

Tampering with Willey

Similar to the Troopers' allegations, Kathleen Willey claimed there was an attempt to influence her Jones deposition and change her story that President Clinton groped her. The alleged conflict centered around Nathan Landow, a multimillionaire Maryland developer, who is a Gore loyalist and a top Gore supporter. His family had ties to the Clinton White House. His daughter, Harolyn Landow, volunteered in the White House social office and Harolyn's husband served as executive director of the initial Presidential Legal Expense Trust (McDonald, "A Gore moneyman at sex scandal's center").

On October 6, 1997 Landow arranged for a chartered plane to fly Willey from her home in Virginia to his estate on Maryland's Eastern Shores where she stayed for two days (Yost, "President denies Willey accusation"). He also contacted Willey many times in the weeks before and after her Jones deposition. Willey claimed that Landow pressured her to renounce her story in the Jones case and testify that Clinton did not grope her. Willey also asserted that Landow offered her a Christmas shopping trip in exchange for her compliance ("Clinton Friend Under Scrutiny"). Landow, of course, denied the allegations.

This is serious. If true, Landow probably committed obstruction of justice or witness tampering. Let's just assume for a moment the allegation is true. What reason did this affluent, powerful, well-connected man have to break the law? There is only one reason I can think of and that is Landow's most powerful connection, President Clinton, needed help. Jones' lawyers subpoenaed Willey trying to prove a pattern of sexual harassment on the part of Clinton. Sure, Willey was not the only person who claimed to be sexually assaulted or harassed by Clinton, but her retraction would have been a major blow to the Jones team. Bill Clinton would have benefited substantially. If Willey's allegations have merit, then odds are Landow did not just pick the paper up one day, notice that President Clinton was in trouble, and figure he would help the most powerful man in the world by changing an accuser's testimony. No, chances are a top Clinton advisor or friend sought out Landow. This could mean the President of the United States was involved in a scheme to obstruct justice to save himself.

As youngsters, my peers and I, always wanted to win in our athletic endeavors. We wanted more than anything to get that clutch hit or drain the shot with seconds ticking. Along the way, most of us learned winning was not everything. We should practice hard and try our best. There were limitations, however, on what our skills could accomplish and also on what we would do to prevail. We all came to understand this: no paying off umpires, no tampering with the clock. Dishonestly winning a game was not worth it. I reckon the Clintons are not big fans of athletics. Bill did get to call the World Series winners and occasionally Hillary Clinton would brandish a baseball cap to remind voters of her new residency, but their hearts were not in it. The Clintons do thrive on another sport. To them politics is akin to a blood sport and they do anything to win. Once they got the home field advantage, there was no stopping them, no restraints as to what they would do to hold onto power. All bets were off.

Tampering with Curie

At the time of Clinton's January 17, 1998 Jones deposition, he had a concocted cover story denying the affair. He used this lie repeatedly in his deposition. Thus he needed Lewinsky and his secretary to corroborate his story otherwise the public would learn he lied. On the night of the deposition, President Clinton contacted Curie and told her to come to his office the next day ("The Starr Report"). The next day he met with Curie and authoritatively issued four statements in a row:

- "'You were always there when she was there, right?'
- 'We were never really alone.'
- 'Monica [Lewinsky] came on to me, and I never touched her, right?'
- 'You can see and hear everything, right?'" (The Starr Report)

Currie believed Clinton sought her agreement. When the authorities asked Clinton about those remarks, he said that he was trying to refresh his memory and find out what she knew ("The Starr Report"). However, Clinton's answer does not make sense. If he wanted to determine her recollections, why didn't he just ask her? Dictating statements to someone does not help to refresh a person's memory. In fact, it may alter one's memory. The pithy, commanding sentences were seemingly designed to tell Curie what his testimony was and what hers should be. If Clinton was alone with Lewinsky, it is absolutely impossible for her to have known what Clinton did with her while alone. Clinton's attempt to persuade a prospective witness, who he frequently referred to in his deposition, to testify falsely seems to resemble witness tampering and/or obstruction of justice ("Opening Statement by Representative Bill McCollum at

Impeachment of William J. Clinton").

By coaching Currie, Clinton assured himself some breathing room and confidence. However, rumors about the sex scandal propagated and finally a stained blue dress was found causing Clinton to publicly admit wrongdoing for the first and only time in his career. If Matt Drudge did not expose the smoking gun, one can only imagine that MonicaGate would have been like every other Clinton misdeed. Clinton would have continued denying it, done everything in his means to prevent the disgrace from going public, and after the "investigative" mainstream media ignored the scandal, it would quietly disappear. The cover up probably would have worked like it always did. Fortunately for Clinton the scandal, while an embarrassment, did not in and of itself involve illegal acts.

The irony here is Clinton went to all this effort to hide the affair, but in reality he did not have to. Clinton's efforts to conceal the affair indicated even he thought it constituted "high Crimes and Misdemeanors." Yet, parents did not. Go figure.

Summary

The worst part of the Clintons' alleged cover up scandals for the young people of our country is not what they did, but the fact that they succeeded and the Clintons were able to get away with them. This gives the children a false sense of security that we can do as we please, then obfuscate and expect to avoid the consequences. I am sure not even a Bill Gates or Jack Welch, let alone your average Joe, could get away with these activities. This is made evident by the trial of rap mogul, Puffy Combs. He is a wealthy and famous personality, but when he allegedly offered his driver a bribe to take responsibility for the gun; he was charged and went to trial. Although Combs was found not guilty, he still was put on trial. In the previously discussed alleged cover up episodes there were no criminal trials. Bill and Hillary Clinton are anomalies, plain and simple, but if kids don't realize this, a future generation may be sucked into a dark trap with "No Way Out."

Not only did the Clintons teach children all of the wrong lessons, they also have significantly lowered the bar for future politicians. The Clintons have set an awful, unethical precedent. It is possible that because of the Clintons, people inclined to a criminal lifestyle, may now consider political careers. Mob leaders like John Giotti eventually get killed, caught, or die in prison. However, politicians like Bill Clinton and his subordinates can essentially investigate themselves through organs of government they control. This conundrum removes pressure on underlings to turn states evidence against corrupt politicians and allows misdeeds to go unpunished. For criminal types not getting caught is paramount, so if they understand they can use the Bill Clinton personal handbook to eschew apprehension, a career in politics may make sense to further their opportunities. Obviously this will mean more corruption in our government that our children and their progeny will have to deal with. Guess who loses out? The ordinary, honest, hard working citizen, like you and me.

Chapter 4
Lying Is OK, As Long As It's About (<u>Fill In The Blank</u>)

Growing up I was a shy kid, so when I started kindergarten my dad offered to pay me what he called "talking up money" as an incentive to participate in class. Everyday I would come home from school, explaining how I participated, and my dad would reward me with some pocket change. I eventually realized I could exaggerate my participation to get an extra shiny nickel and dime. My dad quickly realized I was lying and confronted me. I admitted my guilt. He temporarily discontinued the program, forfeited my largess, and reinforced the significance of honesty and integrity and the consequences of falling short. Losing those earnings was a bitter pill but a valuable lesson.

I learned honesty is very important, which is why I was repeatedly taught to tell the truth at all costs. My parents opined that telling the truth is important in all facets of life. At work you want your word to mean something. You want coworkers to trust and believe you will do what you say when you say that you will do something. It is imperative that this trust exists to avoid tension and an unproductive, inefficient work environment.

My parents said that in personal relationships trust is also important. When you tell your girlfriend you are working late at the office you want her to believe that is where you are, not cheating on her or doing something else. If you have lied to her before, she will suspect you. Even if you are doing what you said, this will lead to friction and compromise the relationship.

A history of truthfulness is important in a difficult situation when one is falsely accused of doing something improper. For example, you are working late at the office when an interloper enters the building and steals money. The authorities investigate, but only scant evidence of a break in is found. The trusted employee would have far less explaining to do than one who lacks veracity. The truthful employee can go home, have a good night sleep, and forget about the whole thing. To the contrary, the untruthful employee will have his story questioned and suspicion cast on him all because of a reputation of fabrications.

An impeccable reputation for honesty takes years to establish and only seconds to destroy, but it is worth the effort to maintain. The Clintons teach us the faulty lesson that you can be treated as an honest person even when you have a reputation for making false, misleading statements. For example, we know that Mrs. Clinton was not candid in the remarks she made about TravelGate and the Castle Grande deal. We also know that Bill Clinton mislead the people about his Monica Lewinsky and Gennifer Flowers relationships. Subsequently more accusations were made about Clinton's involvement in an illegal loan and the groping of Kathleen Willey; Clinton, of course, denied the charges. Although "Clinton's an unusually good liar. Unusually good," as Democratic Senator Bob Kerry put it, the public still treated him as if he was honest. Many say since there was no smoking gun, the public should believe him. However, almost anyone else in that same situation, especially a Clinton accuser, would enjoy zero credibility.

TravelGate Testimony

When the initial investigation began into the Travel Office firings, no one knew who ordered the firings. Many people were questioned, including the First Lady who gave a deposition at the White House in 1995. She testified to playing no part in the removal. When asked who ultimately decided to fire the employees, she said Watkins and McLarty made the decision. When asked if she influenced their action she said, "'I don't believe I did, no'" (The Associated Press, "Independent Counsel: Hillary Clinton Gave 'Inaccurate' TravelGate Testimony"). Independent Counsel Robert Ray's report cited eight conversations between the First Lady and senior White House staff and advisers regarding the firing of the Travel Office workers. There also surfaced a Watkins memo indicating he had to fire the workers as per Mrs. Clinton's wishes. Ray did not think her erroneous statements constituted perjury because Mrs. Clinton might not have realized her conversations were interpreted as an order to fire them. Ray did deem her testimony "'factually inaccurate'" (The Associated Press, "Independent Counsel: Hillary Clinton Gave 'Inaccurate' TravelGate Testimony").

Ray's ruling was disingenuous. Hillary Clinton is a political mastermind who, while still in college, publicly embarrassed Senator Edward Brooke of Massachusetts. She also went to one of the finest law schools in the country, Yale. She is smart and knows the difference between discussing something and giving an order. His decision probably had a lot more to do with political reality.

Not only is Hillary Clinton intelligent, but her testimony coincides with the attitudes held at the Clinton White House. The administration was slow in turning over documents on the firings, fighting the truth at every turn. She had a reason to lie, to protect herself and the administration from the unpopular firings. Although Ray did not indict her, the event demonstrates her lack of integrity. Hillary Clinton could have testified that she discussed the firing of the workers with Watkins and McLarty, but she didn't want her role to be known, so she gave "factually inaccurate" testimony.

Castle Grande Testimony

Similar to the TravelGate scandal, the Clintons camouflaged Hillary's role in the Castle Grande deal. Hillary Clinton testified that she "'didn't know anything about Castle Grande Estates'" ("The Lies of Hillary Clinton"). She also said in an interview with Barbara Walters that she never worked on the Castle Grande project, but she did work on the IDC project, unrelated to Castle Grande. Actually IDC and Castle Grande were basically the same project. Castle Grande was a part of IDC. According to Don Denton, a worker at Madison Guaranty, the project was referred to as Castle Grande by "'everybody who was involved in it'" ("The Lies of Hillary Clinton"). As we already know, Hillary Clinton was involved with it.

Was this another one of Hillary Clinton's honest mistakes? Probably not. She had a definite reason not to be candid. She did not want the public to know she helped fool regulators on a corrupt deal. The two different names were just an excuse when the billing records came up. Presumably she knew what her testimony was referring to; she just didn't want the truth known.

Hillary's Testimony Summary

Trying to hide her role, Hillary Clinton spoke dishonestly about both TravelGate and Castle Grande. When she was trapped, this intelligent woman played dumb, fending naiveté and ignorance of certain facts. Regardless of whether Hillary Clinton deliberately lied or did not know, one must admit there is considerable evidence contrary to her testimony.

Despite this precedent, when subsequent scandals emerge, Clinton supporters say we must take her at her word. For example, when Hillary Clinton denied knowledge of her brother's $400,000 largess for soliciting two controversial pardons, her defenders said we should believe her. My response is, why on earth should we? Her PardonGate statements resembled those other scandals she conveniently deleted from her resumé. She has a pattern of playing dumb about participation in misdeeds when her footprints are all over them. If a memo did appear indicating her involvement, she would most likely just say she did not know the definition of "quid pro quo." No doubt her advocates would buy it.

This teaches the younger generation the lesson it is possible to lie and still be trusted. In today's world that does not happen to everyday people. If children believe lying is no big deal and has no consequences, they will readily lie and think nothing of it. By the time they get questioned by their boss, have a suspicious girlfriend, or get indicted for charges on which they are innocent, it might be too late. Doubts will exist because of their past history. It is hard for the average person to consistently lie and avoid repercussions indefinitely. In fact the only other person I know that obfuscates repeatedly and still maintains a degree of trust is Hillary Clinton's husband, President Clinton.

Gennifer Flowers

During Bill Clinton's presidential campaign, Gennifer Flowers claimed a twelve-year affair with Governor Clinton. Clinton denied Flowers' story. On "60 Minutes" Steve Kroft interviewed Clinton and asked him about the accusation of the affair. In response Clinton said, "'That allegation is false'" ("Gennifer Flowers Questions-#1"). Then Kroft rephrased the question and Clinton responded "'I said that before'" ("Gennifer Flowers Questions-#1"). Sounds like a denial to me.

When Clinton was later deposed he admitted to having sex with Flowers in 1977 ("Clinton's Flowers Testimony"). There is a discrepancy between Clinton's campaign spin and his testimony. The denial during the campaign seems like a blatant lie because he later admitted doing something he previously disavowed. But this is Bill Clinton, who is a master of using misleading language just like his wife did in the two previous examples. According to Clinton logic, Bill Clinton denied a twelve year affair, but never denied having sex with her, so he did nothing wrong and was completely up front with the public. Well, I for one am not impressed. He knew an admission would be the deathknell to his lifelong goal, so he lied and continued to seek the presidency. This shows what an opportunist he is. He did not care what he said and did not care what he did. He just wanted to survive and fight another day, and by his misleading statements he parlayed it into two terms.

Big deal you say. Clinton lied about a twelve year affair. I lied about twenty-five cents in coin. It is all relative. But remember one difference, I got punished, and oh yeah, I was five!

Monica Lewinsky

Although everyone knows this scandal, it is essential to my point, so I'll be as pithy as possible. Monica Lewinsky was a young intern who claimed an affair with President Clinton. The Clinton White House demonized Lewinsky as a lying, obsessed stalker and proclaimed the affair never happened. As we all know on January 17, 1998 President Clinton testified that he did not have "'sexual relations'" with Ms. Lewinsky ("The Starr Report"). As we later learned, Bill Clinton was neither frank with the public nor the courts.

Now you can spin this how you like. You can say it depends on the definition of sex. Such parsing of words, however, is unpresidential and childish. The average child learns it is unacceptable and stops. I know I did. At the tender age of three I sat in the backseat of my family's car and stuck my tongue out at my mom. My mom told me to stop sticking out my tongue to which I retorted, "I did not stick out my tongue. It fell out." My parents laughed at my flimsy excuse, but they did not buy it. They tried even then to instill in me the importance of taking responsibility for my actions, how it builds character. I am not saying I appreciated it then, but I understand it now. Many parents were too willing to accept "baby boy Clinton's" explanation.

You can rationalize that everyone lies about sex. Maybe some people do lie about sex, but we should expect more integrity from the most powerful man in the world. Not only that, but the people who do lie about sex are not making pronouncements to the general public and are not usually preventing someone from a having a fair day in court.

The day before Clinton left office he made a deal with Independent Counsel Robert Ray and admitted that he "'tried to walk a fine line between acting lawfully and testify falsely'" and that his "'responses to questions about Ms. Lewinsky were false'" (King, "Clinton admits misleading testimony avoids charges in Lewinsky probe"). Ray's ruling was quite generous. I was brought up that there are lies and the truth with nothing in between. As far as I am concerned, Bill Clinton committed perjury. He knew if he were truthful, the Jones' lawyers would have had an easier time proving their case of sexual harassment. Maybe the tide would have turned and Clinton's aides and those reluctant to come forward with information would have jumped ship. Many inauspicious things might have happened if Clinton had been truthful, so he was not. He gave fallacious testimony to thwart the Jones team, helping himself at her expense.

His misleading testimony had at most a nominal negative effect on him. Yes, he was impeached, but with his spinners and the liberal network news feeding out of his hand, Clinton's popularity surged. Clinton was not removed from office. It was actually two prominent Republicans who resigned from their jobs during the impeachment proceedings once their infidelities were exposed. It was Independent Counsel Starr who perhaps had his chance of being nominated to the Supreme Court one day thwarted because he took the job of investigating the Clintons. Yes, it is fair to say that Clinton walked away unscathed. While Clinton was fundraising and schmoozing with celebrities, the House Impeachment Managers were fighting for their congressional seats. Clinton's punishment is nothing, a five-year suspension of his law license and a $25,000 fine. He has unlimited earning potential, and besides he intends to give speeches, not practice law. Unfortunately, House Manager Rogan who lost his job trying to uphold justice doesn't have the same earning capacity.

Summary

Clinton spoke dishonestly to get ahead. When Clinton campaigned for president, he promised middle class tax cuts. This stance helped him gain votes by allowing him to attack President Bush's reluctant tax increase. Once president he abandoned the policy and raised taxes. This is similar to Clinton's denying his relationships with Gennifer Flowers and Monica Lewinsky only to admit them later.

In the area of speaking the truth, Mr. Clinton is our worst role model. My parents told me lies would eventually be found out, making the situation worse for the liar. Bill Clinton's untruthful statements did not negatively effect him. Clinton supporters said we should continue to trust the president even though there were numerous reasons not to. Clinton supporters believe President Clinton and expect the public to believe him also, but why should we after Flowers and Lewinsky, to name a few? These are examples of Clinton denying the truth to avoid punishment. This is similar to his response to the Willey claim, denying an accusation. The only difference is no tapes and no stained dresses to support Willey's claim. Consequently Clinton will never admit it, and the public will never know whether it is definitely true.

As we know the scandals involving Clinton are not just about sex, and the misdeeds Clinton denies are not just about sex either. Earlier in the book Governor Clinton's alleged involvement in an illegal loan was described. Three witnesses supported this allegation, James McDougal, David Hale, and Trooper L.D. Brown. But of course Clinton denied the allegation. Again Clinton's liberal proponents said he should be trusted even though he has lied so many times. Why would he not also prevaricate about this scandal? We learn at a young age the expression, "Where there is smoke there is fire." Despite repeated scandals, dubious denials, many people continue to believe him. This sends the awful message to children, if confronted with a difficult situation, just lie. Even if caught, there will be virtually no consequences. In the real world it is impossible to not feel the repercussions of being dishonest unless your last name is Clinton.

Unlike the Clintons, the average citizen can not count on the media to constantly bail us out and will thus suffer the comeuppance of equivocation.

Chapter 5
Don't Be Consistent

Trustworthiness not only involves keeping my word, but also being consistent. My parents said once I found a fixed set of values and opinions on issues, I should not act contradictory to them. If a person keeps changing his thoughts on a subject, after awhile people will start to become skeptical as to whether that person knows what he is talking about. Switching sides without a valid reason makes a person look either opportunistic or uninformed, depleting credibility. My parents told me that it was imperative for me to research issues and opinions to find the side I support and stick with it, so people will understand I mean what I say. They knew opinions would change as my breadth of knowledge grew. What they were advising against, of course, was flip-flopping on issues for the sake of expediency.

Bill Clinton and his White House staff have changed their stance on many key issues for the sole purpose of benefiting the administration. The Clinton administration spinners have said one thing and later said the exact opposite. They were inconsistent, but this did not result in a major outcry, nor did it seem to affect their credibility with the public.

Fingerprints

The death of top White House aide Vince Foster was suspicious in part because of his close friendship with the Clintons and his intimate knowledge about numerous scandals. Maybe he was going to come clean. Maybe he was going to start talking. Maybe that was why he "committed suicide." The suicide scene did not alleviate the skepticism because authorities never found a bullet, little blood was at the scene, and his shoes after walking through a park were not dirty (Blumenfeld, "Vince Foster: Lest We Forget"). Days after the death, a torn up suicide note was found in his briefcase. The note created more suspicion because it had not been found in initial searches and although torn into twenty-eight pieces, it did not have Foster's fingerprints (Burton, "The Death of Vincent Foster").

Was the note a forgery intended to cover up? What exactly would planting a suicide note cover up anyway? The note was found in the White House, so who besides the Clintons, their subordinates, and their friends would be able to plant it in Foster's office? Pressure and suspicion were mounting.

Various Clinton administration officials said the absence of Foster's fingerprints was not unusual because "fingerprints do not attach themselves easily to paper" (Burton, "The Death of Vincent Foster"). This position helped to support the authenticity of the suicide note and discredit the conspiracy theorists.

When Hillary Clinton's subpoenaed billing records were finally found in her book room with her fingerprints on them, however, White House lawyers told the public Hillary Clinton had looked at the billing records during the 1992 campaign and had not seen them since. They said her fingerprints were on the records from that review, and fingerprints can stay on documents for years (Burton, "The Death of Vincent Foster). This spin helped to clear the First Lady from wrongdoing.

One can say the Clintons had nothing to do with the billing records and with the Foster note, but their spinning surrogates certainly were not consistent. When the Clinton team needed fingerprints to be rare and transient, they were, and when the Clinton team needed fingerprints to be rampant and eternal that also worked.

Lewinsky

One of President Clinton's biggest inconsistencies was his contradictory reference to the Monica Lewinsky scandal. He spun the affair as a major public issue when convenient, and called it private when that became more opportune.

President Clinton sought executive privilege to prevent his top aides, Bruce Lindsey and Sidney Blumenthal, from answering questions regarding Monica Lewinsky. Executive privilege is a special prerogative giving the president the right to keep discourse with his aides secret. However, executive privilege does not apply to all issues. Courts have upheld executive privilege claims to protect military and diplomatic issues, law enforcement, and the process of making public policy. In reference to Clinton's executive privilege plea, Viet Dihn, an associate professor at Georgetown University Law Center, said, "'It is being asserted in an area that deals not even with official policy much less national-security policy'" (Grier, "A President's Right to Secrecy").

Mark Rozzell, a political scientist at American University, said, "'Executive privilege must be reserved for the most compelling circumstances and for official governmental matters, not personal matters'" (Marcus, "Constitutional Clash Evokes Watergate Era"). Judge Norma Halloway agreed with the opinion of Rozzell and others rejecting President Clinton's claim (Marcus, "Constitutional Clash Evokes Watergate Era").

The rejection of the claim is irrelevant. By invoking executive privilege to prevent testimony in the Lewinsky matter, he inferred that the affair was an important public issue. That is the relevant point.

When President Clinton was denying the affair, it was imperative that his top aides with intimate knowledge supported his claim. Depending on his aides was risky because if they denied the affair, they might be committing perjury. Thus, a chance existed they would jump ship at the last minute and testify against Clinton. The best way President Clinton could stop his aides from testifying against him was to make sure they did not testify at all. Although the executive privilege request was unsuccessful, Clinton had nothing to lose and much to gain by trying.

Clinton was eventually presented with indisputable evidence confirming the Lewinsky affair, so he had to admit it. With the truth revealed, he moved into damage control. To insure that the American people forgave him and moved on, he spun the scandal differently. He declared the affair an ordinary private indiscretion that he would work out privately with his family. Clinton knew he was not candid with the public and could face a serious backlash. If he could convince the public it was a private issue, he would be politically safe.

In his August 17, 1998 address to the nation he did just that, admitting the relationship with Monica Lewinsky, President Clinton said, "I answered their questions truthfully, including questions about my private life, questions no American citizen would ever want to answer" ("Address to the Nation on Testimony Before the Independent Counsel's Grand Jury"). Later in the address, Clinton reverted to the private issue when he said:

"Now this matter is between me, the two people I love most, my wife and our daughter, and our God. I must put it right, and I am prepared to do whatever it takes to do so. Nothing is more important to me personally. But it is private. And I intend to reclaim my family life for my family. It's nobody's business but ours. Even Presidents have private lives. It is time to stop the pursuit of personal destruction and the prying into private lives and get on with our national life" ("Address to the Nation on Testimony Before the Independent Counsel's Grand Jury").

Clinton hoped to make the Monica Lewinsky issue a private one, so people would see it as a family matter rather than the chief law enforcer's possible attempt to obstruct justice. This tactic worked with the help of a couple of diversionary attacks on hapless third world countries.

This was a classic Clinton example of his consistent inconsistencies with the Lewinsky issue. When Clinton needed to prevent testimony, he made the issue a major public one. When he was caught and sought forgiveness for his error in judgment, the issue became private.

The Power of Material Goods

On numerous occasions President Clinton and his allies tarnished the credibility of informants and accusers. One of the easiest ways Clinton did this was criticizing the money whistle-blowers received.

The Clinton campaign used this tactic efficaciously when Gennifer Flowers sold her story to the <u>Star</u>. The campaign attacked her motives. In the eyes of the Clinton team her goal was to make money and get publicity by trashing the candidate, not of course to make the public aware of the candidate's sleaze. They came up with the term "'cash for trash'" ("Interview James Carville"). Carville described it as "The strategy was to say that there was a lot of money that was passing hands here. It was all odd that this was coming up around 10 days before the election. The strategy was pretty obvious, and I think the strategy worked pretty good" ("Interview James Carville").

As Carville said, rather than deal with the accusation, the campaign attacked the money she received in order to successfully discredit her story and unify support for Clinton. I don't understand what's wrong with her selling her story. If her story is worth a $150,000, that is how much she should get. Clinton's criticism and the term "cash for trash" infer that the money influenced and created the story. Clinton's team persuaded people that the story was about money, not about sexual infidelity or about negative personality traits (such as conniving, lying, and deceit), which are obviously not characteristics we want in elected officials. Clinton and his allies used similar tactics in TrooperGate and MonicaGate to attack the motives of those who made public the scandals.

Clinton apologists were not as concerned when expectant Clinton informers received perks that could be perceived as encouraging silence. For example, when Nathan Landow arranged a chartered flight for Kathleen Willey to stay at his estate for a few days, no objections were forthcoming. Although this service is not a six figure check, it is not ordinary. No well connected, powerful, big shot ever called and arranged a chartered flight to a mansion to wine and dine me. I am sure I am not alone in that regard. Willey has stated during her stay at the estate, Landow tried to get her to change her story. Even if the Clinton team did not set up this little vacation, they certainly learned about it at some point. Yet, there was never any conjecture about anyone's motives in this case. No surprise, the asset exchange argument could go either way depending on if the goal was to discredit someone or to seek a retraction of an accusation.

Book Deal

Another Clinton inconsistency revolved around the lucrative $8 million book deal publisher Simon & Schuster gave Hillary Clinton. The deal seemed hypocritical in light of the outrage liberals expressed when Newt Gingrich got a $4.5 million book deal from HarperCollins (Regnery, "Mrs. Clinton's Book Deal"). In reference to Newt's book deal, President Clinton said "[I don't] even know how to think in these terms" ("Recovered history-What various people said when Newt Gingrich got $4.5 million in book deal").

Besides criticizing the large amount of money that Gingrich was to receive, Democrats were also critical because HarperCollins' owner, Rupert Murdoch, had regulatory issues involving Fox television pending before the government, which the liberals saw as a possible attempt to influence regulators. An ethics investigation ensued, causing Gingrich to nullify the deal and accept a one dollar advance (Regnery, "Mrs. Clinton's Book Deal").

Although the Clintons raised issues about this money, Hillary Clinton, as Senator-elect, had no problem signing a book deal worth much more. The deals were similar. Both involved big money and both could be seen as possible conflict of interests and attempts to exert influence. Viacom owns Simon & Schuster along with CBS, Paramount Pictures, and Showtime. Viacom has regulatory disputes pending before federal agencies (Regnery, "Mrs. Clinton's Book Deal"). A New York Times editorial said, "The deal may conceivably conform to the lax Senate rules on book sales, though even that is uncertain...No lawmaker should accept a large, unearned sum from a publisher whose parent company, Viacom, is vitally interested in government policy on issues likely to come before Congress" (The New York Times editorial, "Mrs. Clinton's Book Deal").

The New York Times and others were concerned Mrs. Clinton's contract violated Senate rules that book deals be "'usual and customary'" (Regnery, "Mrs. Clinton's Book Deal"). It seems Mrs. Clinton's advance failed to meet this qualification. At the time, Pope John Paul II was the only person with a bigger book deal. His book was published worldwide in many different languages. To justify compensating an $8 million advance she must sell over two million copies, a feat which no political book, memoir, or autobiography has ever accomplished (Regnery, "Mrs. Clinton's Book Deal"). It does not sound usual and customary to me!

Hillary Clinton's arrangement was also unusual because standard practice for publishers requires lengthy, detailed proposals from writers to indicate the book's contents. Simon & Schuster admitted to never receiving a written proposal from Hillary Clinton and does not know exactly what it bought the rights to (Regnery, "Mrs. Clinton's Book Deal").

The possible conflict of interest, the outrageously magnanimous advance, and the lack of a proposal raised issues I am sure would have incensed the Clintons, if a Republican politician had made this book deal. Like the other inconsistencies the book deal was not a mistake or change in reasoning. Clinton used the Gingrich book deal fiasco to regain momentum for himself and his party after a disastrous first two years of his presidency. Two years that featured failures like Waco, gays in the military, TravelGate, Hillary Care and Whitewater culminating with the Democrats losing control of the House of Representatives.

When the Clintons were about to leave the White House, they needed money to pay their legal fees and to continue a lavish, celebrity lifestyle; so Senator-elect Hillary Clinton consummated a profitable book contract. The money has helped to make the freshman senator a major player. No spin can justify the Clintons' contrary perspectives on similar book deals.

Summary

The Clinton inconsistencies were merely self-serving, not principled. If they needed the sky to be blue one day and black the next, so be it. There is no shame or disgrace in changing an opinion, we all do it. "We live and learn" as the expression goes. It is when the motive becomes save oneself at any cost, even if it means destroying someone else, that simply flies in the face of parental teachings and acceptable behavior. The Clintons made it an art form.

Chapter 6
Don't be Loyal

No, I am not talking about having affairs, although I just as easily could. I'm referring to Bill Clinton's lack of loyalty to his friends and government workers. Both situations speak to the character of our former president. He puts himself and his own interests over anyone else.

My parents said not every one I meet, for whatever reason, is going to like me; it is human nature. The majority of people I would encounter would be polite and friendly. Some of these people would become close friends on whom I could depend through good and bad times. I was told to respect and be nice to everyone I met, but I should treat those close friends with special care. Those friends are rare and I should be especially grateful for them. I should recognize their efforts and offer them the same unswerving dependability, never forgetting my roots and those who helped me along the way. My parents taught me to be loyal and helpful to those people who went out of their way for me.

Bill Clinton did not do this. He used the reputations of others to help his own reputation and credibility, often exploiting and manipulating close aides and friends. Bill Clinton used them to spread his own lies. By using them in this way he jeopardized their future careers. I am sure people in the Nixon White House who had nothing to do with the scandal had their careers sidetracked because they just worked in the wrong place at the wrong time. Obviously lying for the president is worse. Clinton was not loyal even to associates who worked hard to get him elected and make his presidency a success. He had no qualms taking advantage of his friends and using them as pawns, if it could help him appear innocent.

Paul Begala

Paul Begala worked hard to help Clinton's campaign. Begala was rewarded with a position as a top Democratic National Committee strategist. After the 1996 reelection, Begala accepted a job at the White House. His job deteriorated into spinning scandals to reporters and talk show hosts. With respect to the Monica Lewinsky allegation, Clinton told Begala it was false. In turn, Begala "berated reporters for rushing to judgment and feasting on improper leaks from prosecutors" (Kurtz, "The Defenders").

Begala made the mistake of taking the president at his word. Begala put his own reputation on the line to defend the president. At the time it probably did not seem like too risky of a call, believing President Clinton. One would assume at the very least the President of the United States would be candid with his own top aides and friends.

However, Clinton was not. Clinton knew he had wronged in the Lewinsky matter and that the truth was starting to catch up to him. He most likely feared the truth and its possible repercussions, so he wanted to do whatever he could to keep the public's confidence in his denial. He probably thought that if he could rally his aides and friends to his defense, he would win public trust. Clinton did just that with Begala. He did not care that if the truth came out, it risked hurting the reputation of Begala. He was willing to compromise

Begala's credibility in a conflict solely of his own making rather than take responsibility for his inappropriate, immature behavior.

Clinton took advantage of Begala and abused his trust. This lack of loyalty is unacceptable. After all, Begala is not some random guy who Clinton picked up off the street and benevolently gave a prestigious government job. Begala's intelligence and diligence played a pivotal role in electing President Clinton.

Begala was disappointed when he learned Clinton lied to him. He said, "'I'm not making any bones about the fact that I was angry and disappointed'" (Kurtz, "The Defenders"). Begala told one friend, "'He looked me in the eye and lied to me'" (Kurtz, "The Defenders").

Clinton did not empathize with Begala's needs. Begala has a wife and children to support, but Clinton did not seem to care. Begala was lucky in that the mainstream media was very friendly to the Philanderer in Chief and very cynical of Starr, the Independent Counsel; this helped garner public support for Clinton. Unlike some in the Nixon administration, Clinton and his supporters did not have their careers ruined, but this was unforeseeable at the time.

The Cabinet

Paul Begala was not the only person who Bill Clinton deceived. He pulled the same shenanigans with his Cabinet.

In January of 1998 when the Lewinsky allegation was circulating, Clinton held a cabinet meeting where he repudiated the Lewinsky story. Secretary of State Madeline Albright, Commerce Secretary William Daley, Health and Human Services Secretary Donna Shalala, and Education Secretary Richard Riley were sent out to the media to reiterate the denial. When these top aides found out Clinton used them to disseminate lies, many of them were furious (Hunt, "Saga Continues for Some").

Clinton arranged the meeting to have his high profile Cabinet officers publicly negate the allegation. If he could get them to tell his story, the public would be more trusting, and Clinton would be spared political damage. He subrogated the credibility and reputations of his Cabinet members to avoid responsibility for his transgression.

It's impossible to know the tension inside the White House, but there must have been a considerable amount. Getting hung out to dry by any boss is demeaning, but it must be especially so when the President of the United States does it before the entire nation.

Clinton's betrayal of the Cabinet also may have led to a decline in their effectiveness. Odds are after being humiliated, they would be less willing to again stick their necks out for him. Even if the Cabinet did not hold a grudge, there is still a chance they were not as efficient because of their tarnished reputations. These high ranking administration officials must deal with many different powerful people who might put less faith and confidence in their word and commitment.

In spite of it all, the Cabinet members were lucky. The scandal could have brought down Clinton and them with him. All because President Clinton lied about his relationship with Monica Lewinsky in an attempt to hide the truth, so he could maintain power.

Clinton not only abandoned his cabinet and left them swinging in the breeze but more importantly let the American people down. We do not pay billions of dollars so our government can tell us lies, undermine the judiciary, engage in assorted dalliances on company time while ignoring government business. Presidential appointees are not linemen protecting the quarterback. The more time they spent defending or denying presidential peccadilloes of various consequence, the less time they had to do their job of improving and protecting our institutions and our way of life. While Clinton behaved like an over endowed adolescent and his aides defended the inexcusable, I can only imagine what those around the world who wished us no good were thinking.

Other Aides

Clinton was being judged in both the court of public opinion and the court of law. He effectively sent his Cabinet and aides out professing his false innocence. Their public support would have been worthless, however, if they did not follow through and defend Clinton's story to the grand jury. He had to make sure they repeated his denials.

Clinton did this on January 21, 1998 just a few days after the Drudge Report broke the story about the taped conversations of Lewinsky and Tripp. On that morning Clinton had a meeting with his Chief of Staff Erskine Bowles and his two deputies, John Podesta and Sylvia Matthews. According to Bowles, Clinton denied the Lewinsky affair. Podesta corroborated Bowles' account, testifying Clinton said the Lewinsky allegation was untrue ("The Starr Report").

President Clinton also had a similar conversation with Podesta on January 23, 1998. Podesta told the Grand Jury in that discussion Clinton "'said to me that he never had sex with her...he was extremely explicit in saying he never had sex with her'" ("The Starr Report"). Asked to expand on the definition of sex, according to Podesta, Clinton said he had not performed any sort of sex including oral sex with Lewinsky ("The Starr Report").

Clinton also told a more fascinating version of the lie to Sidney Blumenthal. In a January 21, 1998 conversation between Blumenthal and Clinton, Blumenthal testified that Clinton said Lewinsky pursued him but he rejected her advances. Clinton also told his secretary, Betty Curie, that Lewinsky came on to him, but he rejected her demands ("The Starr Report").

Clinton denied the affair to his aides hoping they would spread the lie to the public and to the courts. He wanted these people to finagle investigators for his own protection. There is no other logical explanation. He did not want to take responsibility for his wrongdoing. The independent counsel was investigating the Lewinsky scandal. Consequently Clinton, a lawyer, had to know his aides probably would be subpoenaed. Clinton did not seem to care. He did not want the public to learn the truth. Clinton even admitted he knew his aides might testify. This seemed to constitute witness tampering or obstruction of justice ("Opening Statement by Bill

McCollum at Impeachment of William J. Clinton"). He had much to gain, but his aides had much to lose.

These aides were sent to spread lies to the grand jury. This could have posed serious legal problems for them because knowingly spreading lies to a grand jury is a crime. Although they may not have known the truth, Starr might not have seen it that way and could have possibly indicted them. Establishing their innocence could have cost them plenty of time and money. These aides were especially fortunate the public did not view MonicaGate as seriously as WaterGate. Some might have actually gone to jail. Clinton exploited senior aides and risked serious harm to their standing, so he could hold on to power at all costs.

Conclusion

Bill Clinton manipulated his closest friends, aides, and supporters for his own personal benefit. To prevent Jones' lawyers and the public from finding out the truth about his relationship with the intern, he abused the trust of his most ardent backers. When his own reputation was at stake, he was willing to risk the good names of his associates to preserve his political career.

Actually, the word "willing" is a little too generous for President Clinton. In reality, Clinton expected them to put their reputations on the line for him. If they were not amenable, regardless of past assistance, they were now irreconcilable enemies. George Stephanopoulos best exhibits this. Stephanopoulos joined Clinton's 1992 campaign where his brains and assiduousness played an essential part in getting Clinton elected. However, Stephanopoulos refused to put his reputation on the line to defend Clinton in the Lewinsky matter. Stephanopoulos wrote,

"I refused to vouch for Clinton's credibility, and I couldn't buy the party line that this was more about Clinton's accusers than his own actions-which meant I was the enemy now. That's the way it was with the Clintons: You were either for them or against them...I heard that as far as Clinton was concerned, I was now a nonperson-

my name was not to be mentioned in his presence" (Stephanopoulos 437-8).

Although Stephanopoulos helped make Bill Clinton president, Clinton could not accept that Stephanopoulos would not spread his lies and therefore Stephanopoulos no longer existed.

Clinton not only disregarded the reputation of his aides but also their wallets. Because of his deceit the investigation was prolonged, costing everyone, especially U.S. taxpayers substantial legal fees. Had he not stonewalled every inch of the way, those costs would have been mitigated.

Clinton viewed his friends and aides as his own personal objects to control. It's hard to figure. Here is a man you would not want as a spouse nor trust when the chips are down. He has no loyalty. Certainly you would not have the confidence to purchase a used car from him. Yet for some reason he was acceptable for the most prestigious job in the world, President of the United States. This does not make sense.

I guess the importance of loyalty that was stressed to me while growing up is not that important anymore. I mean, if the President of the United States is disloyal, maybe disloyalty and back stabbing are what it takes to succeed. There is a significant problem with that reasoning. As president, he was in a position to significantly assist or hinder many people personally and professionally. Therefore, if you knew him, it was best to be on his good side because it could make a great difference in your life. His friends and associates understood this, I'm sure, and preferred to focus on his more favorable personality traits, like his charm and intelligence. The average citizen is not in this special situation. If I am disrespectful and exploit my friends, the odds are they will avoid me and I will have problems making new ones. In Clinton's case there was a definite incentive for these friends to stay on the ship, even in rough waters.

Chapter 7

Treat Others How You Don't Want To be Treated

When President Clinton admitted to the Lewinsky affair, he called for an end to "personal destruction." I do not agree with Clinton's referring to an investigation into irresponsible behavior, abuse of power, perjury, and obstruction of justice as "personal destruction." Groundlessly attacking a prosecutor for trying to do his job of upholding justice, does fit my definition. Independent Counsel Starr received this relentless borking. Starr was one of the many so-called Clinton haters appointed to determine the truth about our president and received a barrage of verbal insults. Some even received threats.

A striking difference emanates between what my parents said and the Clinton philosophy. My parents' lesson was to treat others the same way I want to be treated. If I want people to treat me with respect, I must show them respect. Not only that, my parents told me if I am ever falsely accused, I should be vigorous in my defense, but respectful and not behave as if I had something to hide.

The Clintons have a different policy with regards to whistle-blowing. They called for its end when Clinton's actions were investigated ("personal destruction"), but ignored it when Clinton and his cohorts attacked those trying to expose the truth.

Clinton's character assassinations against informers were inappropriate. Why did he do this? What was he hiding? This attack the messenger mantra made me suspicious there was more than partisan politics behind the various allegations.

FileGate

One way the Clinton team attacked and threatened was by digging up dirt on the opposition, which they apparently used to prevent information from being released or to discredit the source. Using private investigators is not illegal, but inappropriately viewing FBI files is a serious crime. It seems the Clinton White House was guilty of this. In 1993 and 1994 the White House Personnel Security Office requested over nine hundred FBI files of prominent Republicans who no longer worked in the White House. The files included those of prominent leaders, former Secretary of State James Baker, former National Security Advisor Brent Scowcroft, and former CIA Director Robert Gates ("FBI Files Flap").

Craig Livingstone, head of the White House Office of Personnel Security, was at the center of this FileGate scandal. Livingstone, a former Georgetown bouncer, once threatened to attack his female neighbor if she did not silence her dog. Livingstone admitted to frequently using illegal drugs until 1985. Sears fired Livingstone for merchandise irregularities and another company fired him because the employer doubted Livingstone's academic credentials ("The Livingstone Standard").

The other key figure in the scandal, Tony Marcera, has a questionable past. Dennis Casey, a former Gary Hart campaign worker, accused Marcera of stealing $200 from the Hart campaign's petty cash box. Marcera denied the accusation but admitted "'some negative information'" existed in his background regarding work with the Texas Attorney General's office ("The Livingstone Standard").

There are many questions that I want to ask. Why in the world would a person with a tainted record like Livingstone be given a job at the White House? It doesn't make sense that Livingstone could not hold a job at Sears but was a superb choice for the head of the White House Office of Personnel Security. Although his past should seemingly prevent him from such a job, Livingstone received this prestigious position. Obviously, someone must have wanted him and had the power to hire him. Although I don't have Livingstone's questionable background, it is fairly certain I would have been turned down for the position of head of the White House Personnel Office. Maybe that's it. Maybe his questionable past made him a prime candidate for the position, but who had the authority to make such a questionable call?

Hillary Clinton was one person who had the influence. According to Gary Aldrich, former FBI agent, White House Associate Counsel William Kennedy confirmed that Hillary orchestrated the hiring of Livingstone. Aldrich alleged that Livingstone admitted this directly to him and his partner ("Author of "Unlimited Access" Says Hillary hired FileGate figure, Craig Livingstone").

Aldrich's partner, Dennis Sculimbrene independently confirmed Aldrich's statement. Sculimbrene claimed Nussbaum told him that Livingstone got his job because of the First Lady. The sworn affidavit of Deborah Perroy, a member of the National Security Council support staff, also confirmed Hillary Clinton's involvement. A separate affidavit by Sheryl Hall, a former White House computer specialist, confirmed Perroy's affidavit. Hall said she "'understood that Craig Livingstone was brought to the White House by Mrs. Clinton and that Mr. Livingstone spoke for Mrs. Clinton…Consequently, to oppose a request or instruction from Livingstone was to oppose Mrs. Clinton'" ("Inside the Clinton White House").

Dick Morris was quoted in the diary of Sherry Rowlands, a Washington call girl, as implicating the First Lady's involvement in FileGate ("FBI Files Flap"). Maybe being a call girl doesn't give her the most credibility, but she wrote it in her diary. Why would anyone fabricate in her own personal diary?

Linda Tripp also testified that she believed that the White House uploaded FBI files to share them with the Democratic National Committee at the order of Mrs. Clinton ("Hillary Clinton: "I'm Too Important to Testify").

The ex-wife of Bill Kennedy alleged that her former husband took FBI files home and transferred their contents onto his laptop computer. Mrs. Kennedy believed that Mrs. Clinton was involved with the plot and the files were intended to make the information available to the Clinton administration (Novak, "'Filegate' ready to swing open").

Sworn evidence implicated Mrs. Clinton in FileGate. Further proof of her relationship with Livingstone was his frequent visits. Livingstone bragged about his access to the White House residence and Secret Service logs corroborated this ("Hillary Clinton: "I'm Too Important to Testify").

Evidence tied Hillary Clinton to the scandal, but she adamantly denied both involvement in the scandal and with the hiring of Livingstone. No surprise here because remember she denied involvement in Castle Grande and TravelGate too. Let's look at possible motives. Did Hillary Clinton have a reason to access the FBI files? I think she did. Hillary knew the scandals left behind in Arkansas and probably knew more would come. If Republicans got close to the truth, this FBI information could discredit those possible whistle-blowers. This, of course, would have benefited the Clinton administration.

If Hillary Clinton were involved in this scandal, she would have had a reason to deny it. The Clintons never admit wrongdoing. So what's new here? By stalling, stonewalling, and obfuscation, they repeatedly saved their political careers. Why not do it again? The Clintons had a motive to illegally access FBI files and lie about it.

What motives did these aforementioned people have to claim Hillary Clinton's involvement in FileGate? Was it money? Was it fame? Was it a desire to expose the truth? I don't think there was enough fame or money in this to offset the slings and arrows they could expect directed their way once they crossed the Clintons. For those who testified under oath there was also the little matter of perjury, which not everyone treats as cavalierly as the Clintons. Quite simply they had nothing to gain and a lot to lose.

The Clinton White House response to the FileGate scandal was dubious at best and raised more suspicion of the First Family. The White House's inappropriate possession of FBI files was first divulged when the White House referred to Billy Dale's FBI file to justify his firing from the travel office. The White House claimed it obtained Dale's file from the White House archives to complete background information. The public then learned the White House actually requested Dale's file from the FBI seven months after his firing. The White House retorted that the General Accounting Office (GAO) sought the file for an investigation into the Travel Office firings. A claim the GAO denied (Coulter 137). The White House then said Dale's file was one of a couple hundred accidentally acquired FBI files. The White House claimed the FBI files were not politically based because the names just went alphabetically to the letter "G" (Coulter 138).

The White House made a good point. If a person wanted to dig up dirt on the opposition or find information for blackmailing someone, that person would want information on all perceived threats, not just up to "G." Therefore, it was no surprise later when the public learned the list went well beyond "G" (Coulter 138).

Clinton's next excuse dismissed the files as a "'bureaucratic snafu'" (Coulter 139-140). The White House claimed that the Secret Service gave an outdated employee list to the security office. However, two Secret Service agents, John Libonati and Jeffrey Undercoffer refuted the White House's claim (Coulter 140).

The Clinton White House's obtaining FBI files of prominent Republicans was reminiscent of WaterGate. Democratic candidates could have been given dirt on opponents. The possibility for the misuse of the FBI files was boundless. President Clinton knew the seriousness of having the files. Several different reasons were offered for having them. All were summarily shot down. Why would

President Clinton set out explanations so easily refuted, with so much at stake? Perhaps because the true explanation was the obvious one. Sometimes what you see is what you get. Besides he had so much success by throwing up smoke screens. Why would this be any different?

The Senate Judiciary Committee learned a six month hiatus existed in the log recording of the FBI files, who checked out what and when. Livingstone claimed that the log wasn't kept for the months of March to September of 1994. However, Livingstone's assistant, Mari Anderson, contradicted Livingstone. In a deposition, Anderson claimed she did keep the log and it had vanished. This raises the question, who saw the files? ("The Six-Month Gap").

Overwhelming evidence pointed to wrongdoing. We knew Livingstone and Marcera wrongly obtained FBI files, the White House gave invalid excuses, records of who saw the files disappeared, and numerous people implicated Hillary Clinton. We knew all this, but no one was indicted and no one went to jail. More smoke ascended to the heavens than that caused by the Sierra Club's anti-forest thinning policies. Yet, authorities never discovered the fire.

This gives a young person a faulty impression of our legal system. If I owned a local nightclub and the authorities caught my friend with a FBI file on the owner of a competitor's club, they would probably arrest him for having the FBI file. He could claim that he accidentally acquired it, that excuse probably would not go too far. The prosecutor might try to cut my friend a plea bargain seeing the logical connection between my club and the competition. The prosecutor might try to get my friend to testify about my part in the plot, in which case I would end up in trouble. Regardless of convictions, there would be arrests and prosecutions. That is what happens in our country to people who get caught breaking the law. Well, everyone except Bill Clinton and company.

Charles Colson from the Nixon era went to jail on charges related to FBI file possession. Livingstone was never charged with any violations of law. No pressure was ever put on him to cop a plea to implicate superiors. The mainstream media basically ignored the story. This allowed Filegate to be dismissed as "bureaucratic snafu" and to slowly disappear like so many other scandals had without any accountability. This is scary. Two people commit a similar offense, only one goes to jail. How democratic is that?

Attack Ken Starr

Ken Starr was an appellate judge liberals liked. When President Bush nominated Clarence Thomas to the Supreme Court, some liberals said Starr should have received the nomination. When Special Prosecutor Fiske was under attack, both liberals and conservatives lauded Starr as a good replacement. That was the end of Starr's joy ride. Once Starr started actually investigating the Clintons, Democrats vehemently denounced him, thereby damaging his career (Mitchell, "Welcome to the Club!").

James Carville, the 1992 Clinton campaign manager, was the Clinton associate most critical in attacking Starr. In 1996 Carville created the Education and Information Project, a non-profit organization designed to discredit Ken Starr. Carville claimed that Starr was a "bitter partisan" with an anti-Clinton agenda. Carville said, "'This whole thing is a federally funded smear campaign by a man that doesn't have anything better to do than go around and harass women'" (York, "Carville's Cast of Characters").

After founding the EIP, Carville gave many interviews and speeches attacking Starr. Not only did Carville portray Starr as a partisan, but Carville also depicted him as a person obsessed with sex. "'Sex and more sex, that's all it is,'" said Carville (Momenteller, "Big Mouth Carville's Last Stand"). Carville claimed Starr and his assistants only cared about publicity, rather than a serious investigation. Carville's reasoning for the tirade against Independent Counsel Starr was "'Because with $40 million and five years into this, all this man does is pose for pictures and give interviews'" (York, "Carville's Cast of Characters").

Starr could do no right. Clinton's private attorney, David

Kendall, attacked Starr in a fifteen page letter where Kendall accused Starr of leaking secret grand jury testimony to reporters. Kendall said he would seek judicial relief and a contempt of court ruling ("Clinton denies coaching witness; lawyer attacks Starr").

Starr was also criticized for subpoenaing Sidney Blumenthal. On CNN's "Late Edition" Paul Begala said, in reference to Blumenthal's legal fees, "'Sidney and his family were fined $10,000 for the crime of criticizing Ken Starr. And I think that's a chilling, chilling thing.'" In reference to the subpoena of Blumenthal, former White House Counsel Lanny Davis said on "Fox News Sunday" that Starr had put "'a $10,000 tax on his family with legal fees'" (Kurtz, "Starr is Urged to Curtail Inquiry"). Starr subpoenaed Blumenthal because he was a top White House aide who might have knowledge for the investigation, but Starr's critics did not care. Parenthetically they never objected to the legal fees Paula Jones was incurring.

Along with the criticism came the uproar for Starr to resign and for Starr to be investigated. Democratic Senator Patrick Leahy said on NBC's "Meet the Press" that "'Kenneth Starr has gotten totally out of control. He has this fixation of trying to topple the president of the United States. He's doing everything possible to do it'" (Kurtz, "Starr is Urged to Curtail Inquiry'"). Lanny Davis went so far as to say that Starr was "'a prosecutor, in my opinion who has lost all judgment, who is out of control and who I think is guilty of misconduct that needs to be investigated'" (O'Connor, "Clinton Allies Attack Starr Again").

Ken Starr was offered the job of independent counsel. He took the job and did it to the best of his ability. Because his job was to investigate Bill Clinton, the President's subordinates and associates attacked Starr's work viciously. Starr did his job and in turn was called a pervert, a hack, a partisan, a smearer, a deceiver, and an abuser of power. It was Starr's job to find out whether the president broke the law. He adeptly prosecuted, obtaining numerous convictions including that of Arkansas Governor Tucker and the Clintons' friends the McDougals. Once Starr got Tucker, it looked bad for the Clintons, that they themselves might be indicted.

Starr was doing a good job, too good of a job. He had to be undermined and destroyed. This is when the attacks on Starr began to take shape and intensify. The Clinton administration declared war. The Commander in Chief mobilized and deployed the troops. Too bad Clinton didn't spend as much time fighting our nation's enemies as he did his own. The attacks successfully caused the public to doubt Starr's investigation and sympathize with the Clintons as victims.

Whatever the allegations, the Clintons' openly declared their innocence. If they really were innocent, why the time, energy, and executive resources attacking and discrediting Starr? The Clintons probably knew they could be indicted and even go to jail, so they had to make sure it didn't happen. Their strategy put Starr on the defensive with brutal, unjust attacks in order to undermine his authority. Such attacks on a prosecutor are virtually unprecedented.

The attacks did just that; they decreased his effectiveness as a prosecutor. One would think the attacks themselves constituted obstruction of justice because they impeded the investigation. I am sure that if I was a small businessman on trial and had my subordinates and associates relentlessly and groundlessly attack the prosecutor, the intimidation might be seen as an attempt to obstruct justice. People would be able to logically connect the dots between my trial, my associates' attacks on the prosecutor, and the prosecutor losing his effectiveness. The connection seems obvious, but people missed it when the president was the target of the investigation.

The media's coverage kept the public in the dark. The media portrayed the Clintons sympathetically and helped to demonize Starr. According to the mainstream media, Starr's investigation was an unjust political attack, but the Clinton associates' attacks on Starr were okay. So much for objective reporting. That episode is the main reason why Starr, in my opinion, will never be appointed to the Supreme Court bench. The Clintons, however, went on their merry way.

Attack Paula Jones

Paula Jones was a young Arkansas government employee who was summoned by Governor Clinton to a Little Rock hotel room. In the room he allegedly exposed himself and propositioned her. She sued him for sexual harassment (Straub, "What now for Paula Jones?")

Rather than getting proper justice for being harassed by Governor Clinton, she got the justice that befell all living Clinton informants. Her reputation, her integrity, her appearance were attacked and smeared. Everything about her was attacked.

One of the most infamous insults about her was when James Carville called her "'trailer park trash.'" He said, "'If you walk through a trailer park with a $100 bill in the air, you can find all kinds of trash'" (Molchan, "'Trailer Park trash'").

Clinton denied wrongdoing, which is no surprise because he never admitted anything unless his back was up against a wall. If as Clinton said the allegation was false, why didn't Clinton and his allies let her have her fair day in court? If they knew Clinton did no wrong, obviously Jones had no evidence and was just lying. Clinton did not want to deal with the issue in that manner; rather his surrogates went into full attack mode to discredit her. I always thought that waging a campaign of "personal destruction" was inappropriate. According to my parents, it was an extraordinarily bad tactic, people would assume I was covering something up. Regardless of innocence, my parents said that attacking and intimidating was a sleazy tactic and was just the wrong thing to do. The Clinton modus operandi may have been successful most of the time, but it is nothing to be proud of.

Clinton's campaign of personal destruction against Jones worked. It changed her lifestyle and turned many people against her. "'I'm afraid to leave our apartment,' Jones said. 'I rarely go outside even to take the boys for a walk in the stroller. When I go to the grocery store, I wear sunglasses so people won't recognize me'" (Straub, "What now for Paula Jones?").

One would think the sexual harasser would fear going out in

public. One would think the sexual harasser would have to wear sunglasses to elude detection to avoid being jeered. However, thanks to the Clinton team's attacks on Jones, it was she, the victim who had to be wary. These attacks successfully discredited her and again virtually had no negative consequences for the Clintons. There was no public outcry about the intimidation.

For the average person, whose last name is not Clinton, this tactic would have been counterproductive. For example, imagine a manager who sexually harassed a female worker, and then had his friends investigate the victim's past sexual history and verbally derided her. Assume further the evidence might not suffice to prove the manager perpetrated the original harassment. The subsequent events could sway opinion. The manager would be castigated for the attack, thereby making the allegation seem more plausible. The backlash from this might help to sustain the original charges. This defamation tactic, which would not have worked for the manager, worked for Clinton. This sets an awful example for young people because Clinton was in our face everyday for eight years, not like the fictitious manager. Young people too often witnessed the success of Clinton's verbal attacks, rather than its failure for the average person.

Jones was not only verbally attacked, but also the IRS audited her soon after she rejected a settlement. The audit was strange in that Jones' family had little income. The family lived on the $37,000 a year that Jones' husband earned. They did not own a home and only had one car for their four person family. Democratic Representative James Traficant said, "'The IRS did not just target Paula Jones. The IRS is nuking Paula Jones because of the sensitive politics involved'" ("Rep. Traficant on IRS Audits Paula Jones Who Has no Income").

The audit seemed like a deliberate attempt to destroy Jones. I think she was audited so people would not accept her allegation. I find it hard to believe the IRS scrutinized the nearly indigent Jones family without White House intervention when there are so many powerful organizations and people whose finances need examining.

Jones was not the only Clinton enemy the IRS audited. The administration's attempt to destroy Jones was obvious, but the accountability for the "'personal destruction'" of Jones was not.

Attack Monica Lewinsky

When the Monica Lewinsky affair came to light, Clinton denied the affair and attacked Lewinsky, calling her a "'stalker'" ("The Starr Report").

This was the one time character attacks and threats did not work, but for the wrong reasons. The tactic should not have worked because the public should have been outraged that the President of the United States was using what seemed like a Gestapo tactic. The public should have been indignant that Clinton refused to give Lewinsky a fair chance to tell her story. The public should have cried foul when a young female worker allegedly had sex with her boss in his office, and it just so happened that the boss was the most powerful person in the world. Was she compelled to do something that she did not want to do? Was she a victim of sexual harassment? The media should have led a public outcry because the White House spin machine was discrediting her rather than dealing with the allegation. What was he hiding? Why did he have to resort to "'personal destruction'"? The media should have tried to uncover the truth and thwart the character assassination.

This time the verbal attacks against Lewinsky could not work because a stained dress was found. After that discovery there was nothing Clinton and his dream team of spinners could do by way of denial. If that dress had not have been found, the attacks no doubt would have prevailed. We would still be thinking of Lewinsky as an obsessed "stalker" and who knows what other catchy insults Clinton and his allies would have conjured. If that dress had not have been found, probably Lewinsky, like Jones, would be scared to leave her house because the attacks would have turned public sentiment against her. It was this hard evidence that distinguished this episode from all the others.

Kathleen Willey Defamation

Kathleen Willey claimed President Clinton groped her. Once Willey came forward with her disturbing but credible allegation, she was defamed and threatened.

Two months before Willey's deposition in the Paula Jones lawsuit, Willey discovered three car tires had nails in them. Bruce Horlkick, the owner of the Salisbury Tire and Service where Willey brought her car, said that "'masses of nails'" were in the tires and that "'It didn't look like an accident'" (Mostert, "What WAS the "Message" Sent to Kathleen Willey via Car Vandalism, and an Executed Cat?").

A few days after the car incident, Willey's cat mysteriously disappeared. That marked the end of the frightening experiences until January 8, 1998, two days before her testimony in the Jones case. On that day an unknown man allegedly confronted her near her Richmond home. The man knew about the tires and asked if she had gotten them fixed. The man also knew about the missing cat and asked about the cat (Schmidt, "Starr Probing Willey Allegations"). The man inquired about her children by name and said, "'Don't You Get the Message?'" (Mostert, "What WAS the "Message" Sent to Kathleen Willey via Car Vandalism, and an Executed Cat?").

The jogger asked her about the tires and the cat to let Willey know the two episodes were related. The purpose was to intimidate her. The man asked about her children to instill fear in her about their safety. The message was clear: they could steal her cat without detection and would have no problem kidnapping her children. The timing and the frequency disproved random occurrences. Someone cognizant of Willey's situation wanted to silence her.

Clinton had much to gain if Willey recanted her story. Her allegations were similar to Jones' charges. If Clinton could have gotten Willey to change her story, it would have hurt Jones' case. Also, Willey's sexual assault charge against Clinton was possibly a criminal offense. Obviously, Clinton did not want her to testify.

The attempts to thwart Willey's testimony scared her. She saw what had happened and was forewarned what could happen.

Nonetheless, she decided to appear on "60 Minutes" to tell her story. When she did come forward, the Clinton team attacked her credibility, using letters she had written the president.

She wrote him letters requesting work because she was struggling economically ("The Willey Letters"). Why would Willey keep in contact with Clinton after the alleged episode? The simple answer is she desperately needed a job, and who better able to provide one?

In the summer of 1997, Bruce Lindsey, Deputy Counsel to the President, requested the letters Willey wrote to the president soliciting employment. Why did Bruce Lindsey need these private letters? Did Lindsey want the letters in case it was necessary to attack Willey's reputation and credibility? ("Willey Lawsuit").

Testimony in the Judicial Watch's FileGate lawsuit expounded on the release of the letters. In March 1998, the White House realized Willey was going on "60 Minutes." Lindsey told Deputy Counsel Cheryl Mills that the letters were inconsistent with Willey's assertion. The weekend of the show members of the White House Counsel's Office met to discuss the letters. Lindsey, Mills, and White House Counsel Charles Ruff attended the meeting. Lindsey called President Clinton and advised Clinton to release the letters and he acceded. Blumenthal and Hillary Clinton also played a role in releasing the letters ("Willey Lawsuit").

Fearing the political implications of Willey's allegations, the White House used the letters to attack Willey's reputation ("Willey Lawsuit"). The White House hoped to show her continued correspondence and lack of anger proved the accusation false. Once again the Clinton White House was in full attack mode to discredit and intimidate another hapless victim. After all we have learned, I can not imagine anyone subjecting themselves to such an onslaught, if there was no merit to a claim. These tactics that I learned were reprehensible would ultimately succeed with minimal media coverage and no liberal women's group outrage. It was pretty much business as usual.

To make matters worse, Federal District Judge Royce Lamberth ruled the release of the letters by the Clintons and their aides violated the Privacy Act, a federal law (Dougherty, "Judge: Clinton committed 'criminal violation'").

Bruce Lindsey at one point indicated the White House released the documents because it was worried that her allegation would influence or expand criminal investigations into Clinton's activities. Larry Klayman, Chairman of Judicial Watch said, "'The release of Ms. Willey's documents was not only a criminal violation of the Privacy Act but, as Lindsey's admissions confirm, was also part of an effort to obstruct justice, and intimidate a witness in a criminal probe concerning Bill Clinton. Criminal prosecutions are warranted'" ("Judicial Watch-Clinton Lawyer Admits Willey Documents Released to Influence Lewinsky Investigation").

Prosecution sounds to me like it would have been a good idea, when a federal judge says the president violated the law. I guess something was needed, like a Justice Department, to pursue the matter further. The bottom line is this: Did we really need a president and staff spending their time and taxpayer's money on issues like this? Don't the American people deserve better individuals with higher standards in leadership positions?

Intimidate Elizabeth Ward Gracen

Elizabeth Ward Gracen was a television actress who in 1983 allegedly had a brief sexual encounter with Bill Clinton. During the 1992 presidential campaign, Gracen claimed to receive threatening phone calls, that scared her into keeping quiet about the affair. Later her agent met with Hollywood producer and Clinton friend, Harry Thomason, and Clinton lawyer, Mickey Kantor. At this meeting Gracen agreed she would repudiate any relationship with Clinton. This agreement benefited Gracen's career ("Don't You Get the Message"). With regards to her silence, Gracen said, "'I believe if I came out and admitted it, he would never have been president'" (Dunleavy, "Elizabeth Gracen: I was a victim of Clinton's reign of terror").

As Gracen said it is likely that the public's knowledge of her alleged affair with Clinton, coupled with Flowers' allegation, would have terminated Clinton's campaign. The Gracen assertion would have shown a pattern of Clinton's alleged infidelity and thus given more credibility to Flower's accusation. It would have been harder for Clinton to have gained the respect and trust of the American people, and at the very least he would have been forced to spend invaluable campaign time defending himself against the allegations. Threats postponed her coming forward about the affair. Did these alleged threats in effect make Bill Clinton president?

Coincidentally, once the campaign ended and Gracen was no longer a detriment to Clinton, the threats desisted. However, this changed when Jones' lawyers subpoenaed Gracen. Around Christmas time of 1997, Gracen received an anonymous phone call from a man admonishing her to avoid an imminent subpoena ("Actress Who Claimed Sex with Bill Says IRS is Hounding her").

Gracen did not take the call seriously, until the next day when she was subpoenaed in Little Rock, Arkansas. Throughout the ensuing months Gracen's family and friends were harassed. Gracen feared for her safety. Then eight months after the initial warning about the subpoena, the same man called Gracen and instructed her not to talk about Bill Clinton. The man warned about a possible character assassination and an IRS investigation. A couple of weeks later she began receiving IRS letters ("Actress Who Claimed Sex with Bill Says IRS is Hounding her").

While on vacation in St. Martin, three men in suits ransacked her cabana. Nothing was missing. A Rolex and $2,000 in plain view on a coffee table were left untouched. Gracen believed they were looking for damaging evidence that she might have had. The phone calls and the break in left Gracen terrified. Gracen said, "'Yes, I was physically scared. We are talking about the presidency of the country here, and between friendly calls on one hand telling me to get out of town for my own good and then talking about smear tactics on the other, I got scared. Yes, physically scared'" (Dunleavy, "Elizabeth Gracen: I was a victim of Clinton's reign of terror").

When Gracen was in a position to tell the alleged truth and hurt

Clinton, she received threats. The Jones' lawyers sought to establish a pattern of sexual activity, cover ups, and threats. It seems Clinton knew Gracen was a valuable witness and thus he would not have wanted her to testify. The threats were not only immoral but could be construed as obstruction of justice or witness tampering. The connection between the harassment and Clinton seems obvious to me. The threats seem designed to prevent derogatory information about Clinton from coming forward. A connection also possibly exists between the threats and the government. The caller knew a subpoena was going to be issued and knew that she was going to start receiving letters from the IRS. Sounds to me like someone had inside information. Coincidentally, Bill Clinton, the only person who the threats benefited, was rather high up in our government.

There was no serious effort to get to the bottom of these events. There should have been a thorough investigation and indictments if someone was identified. Of course one can assume that all these claims are fabrications without merit. It seems to me that at some point one must conclude there may be merit in some of these allegations. The impressionable young person may interpret this to mean that he also can use this tactic, but he cannot. I'm sure if I were at school verbally threatening a female student, I would be suspended or expelled for sexual harassment and threatening violence—and fast. But when people possibly did it to succor President Clinton in order to thwart an investigation, there were no consequences. The politically correct mantra stopped at Clinton's door.

Sally Perdue Threats

In 1983 Sally Perdue allegedly had an affair with President Clinton. (Limbacher, "Clinton-Connected Bribes, Break-ins, Beatings, Death Threats"). According to Perdue, a Democratic operative warned her not to divulge the affair. The man threatened physical injury ("'Don't You Get the Message'"). Later, Perdue's car window was broken and a spent shotgun shell was discovered on the car seat (Limbacher, "Clinton-Connected Bribes, Break-ins, Beatings, Death Threats").

A woman claimed an affair with President Clinton and then gets threatened, her window broken, and a shotgun shell placed on the seat. I and any other kid would "'get the message'." Someone was blatantly attempting to silence her and show her possible consequences of talking.

In all these aforementioned scenarios there is only one possible benefactor; no one else is ever suggested as having anything to gain. It has to make one wonder about Clinton's truthfulness. The claimed activity ceases when there is cooperation, intensifies when there is not. Do I think Clinton personally engineered these events? I don't know. It could be operatives or Clinton's fanatical supporters or it could be all lies, but it has to make one wonder about Clinton's truthfulness.

If Perdue's allegations were true, the threats she received were successful. They caused her to flee the country, so she would not have to testify. She was scared, so she ran. There may even be more to her story than what is on the record. She was not willing to put her life on the line as she perceived the threat. Again my parents were wrong. Threatening people was not their way to deal with adversaries. They saw such strategies as desperation, illegal, and bound to backfire. They had the naïve belief that the truth would prevail. Of course, it would have been unthinkable to them that the person on the other side of the argument was the President of the United States with unlimited resources at his disposal and no hesitancy to use them.

Threaten Dolly Kyle Browning

Dolly Kyle Browning knew Bill Clinton since she was eleven years old. The two attended high school together and were good friends from the mid 1970's until the early 1990's. According to Browning, their camaraderie included a sexual relationship. Because of Browning's contention she was threatened and defamed

("Amended Complaint").

In January of 1992 Browning became cognizant that The Star was writing an article about her relationship with Clinton. Browning tried to warn Clinton, but he never returned her call. Instead Browning's brother, Walter Kyle, a worker for Clinton's presidential campaign in New Hampshire, called her and instructed her to deny the story. A few days later, Kyle and Browning talked again. In this conversation, Kyle on behalf of Clinton, supposedly threatened Browning saying, "'if you cooperate with the media, we will destroy you'" ("Amended Complaint").

The above exemplifies one of the numerous times that people associated with Clinton threatened Browning. She allegedly received a call from Roger Clinton also pressuring her to refute the story ("Amended Complaint").

After Clinton became president, Browning still occupied the time of his associates. Browning had written a manuscript called Purposes of the Heart based on her long affair with Bill Clinton, though names and location were changed. The White House was concerned about the book. In the fall of 1993, Bruce Lindsay, Deputy White House Counsel, threatened Browning by telling her sister that "'we've read your sister's book and we don't want it published'" ("Amended Complaint").

Bruce Lindsey and Dorcy Kyle Corbin, Browning's sister, came to an agreement regarding the contents of the book as emissaries for Browning and Clinton. Browning could admit to a long term relationship that included sex as long as she did not say "'adultery'" or "'affair.'" If Browning cooperated, the attack dogs would be muzzled ("Amended Complaint").

Browning had information that at the time would have been harmful to President Clinton. Associates threatened her not to talk and successfully delayed Browning's admission of the affair. If Browning had come forward early during the campaign it might have been a disastrous blow to Clinton. If she told the American people the truth, Clinton would have had a difficult time establishing himself as a serious candidate and probably would have become another Gary

Hart. He did not want past activities to get in the way of his life long ambition.

What is the lesson here for our future politicians? It is certainly not, don't act inappropriately and be faithful. More like, threaten your mistress, scare her into silence. I bet after Clinton, Gary Hart would have dealt with his mistress problem a little differently and who knows, maybe he would have gotten the nomination!

The threats were designed to abridge Browning's Constitutional rights. Every American has the right to freedom of speech. Government agents threatened Browning that lies and defamation would be spread about her if she said certain things. Where was the politically correct crowd when you needed them?

After Browning and Clinton's friendship ended, they met again at their thirtieth high school reunion. Clinton and Browning gave different accounts of their conversation. According to Browning, the two sat in front of a large column and the only people within six feet of them were two Secret Service agents except for a brief interruption when Marsha Scott, a Clinton aide, approached them. Browning reminded Clinton of the previous threat, for which he allegedly apologized ("Amended Complaint").

Mr. Clinton claimed that he wrote a memorandum after the conversation with Browning, which differed from Browning's testimony at the Jones trial. Clinton wrote in reference to Browning's manuscript that "'She said she would say it was a fantasy but she needed the money and she didn't care if it hurt me or the presidency, that others had made money and she felt abandoned'" ("Amended Complaint").

Clinton claimed that after he wrote the memorandum, he gave it to Marsha Scott who added to it. Scott wrote "'I stood by the President the entire conversation and heard and watched [Mrs. Browning]…[Mrs. Browning] repeatedly said her story was not true but that she was angry and needed money. [Mrs. Browning] would throw out an accusation and then say it was a lie'" ("Amended Complaint").

Clinton cruelly attacked Browning. From this memorandum,

Clinton and Scott portrayed Browning as a confused, erratic liar. They portrayed her as a self-centered superficial person who would do anything for money. They even depicted her as the aggressor, Mr. Clinton as the innocent victim, quite similar to Clinton's Lewinsky scandal. The above memorandum was designed to discredit Browning and prevent the publication of her manuscript. The problem was that, like the Clinton fairy tale about Lewinsky, it seems the memorandum was not true.

If the account was Browning's word versus that of Scott and Clinton, it would be hard to believe one group over the other because all three could be defending their self-interest. However, other people with no interest in the situation supported Browning's explanation. A few guests at the function submitted affidavits substantiating Browning's testimony. They testified that Marsha Scott was absent during the discourse and thus did not overhear it ("Petition for Order to Show Cause Why William Jefferson Clinton Should Not Be Held in Criminal Contempt of Court").

The evidence indicated Scott prevaricated. What motivated Scott to lie in order to debase Browning? She had no reason. On the other hand, President Clinton did have a motive.

If Browning lied, Clinton would not have needed Scott's help. It would have been a "he said, she said" with some believing him and others her. He would have only needed Scott's help, if Browning's account was true because then he knew other witnesses would support her account (as they did). Therefore for the public to believe him, he would need someone to vouch for him, enter Marsha Scott.

Reporter, Jane Mayer of <u>The New Yorker</u>, also helped to discredit Browning and her manuscript. In a May 26, 1997 article she maliciously attacked Browning, insinuating that the mainstream press blatantly repudiated her story and even Regnery which she characterized as an obscure, extremist, right wing press dubbed her story worthless and refused to publish it. The article was a crippling attack on Browning, but it was not true. Browning never sent a copy of her manuscript to Regnery. Alfred Regnery never saw the manuscript and therefore never expressed those comments

("Amended Complaint").

The content of the article was no accident. Jane Mayer, a Clinton-friendly writer, apparently abandoned journalistic ethics and defamed Browning for her buddy. Her false statements in the article were totally unacceptable, but they helped thwart any possible book deal that Browning's manuscript might have received.

The attacks and threats by Clinton's allies succeeded. Browning became the issue, not the affair. Her reputation and integrity were impugned. Again, same formula, same result. All contrary to the teachings I learned growing up. Little speculation ensued regarding the startling pattern of why anyone who dared to hold the Clintons accountable was inundated in a never-ending sea of "personal destruction."

One of the points I found most disturbing about this sequence of behavior was parents not only refused to question but many were visibly infuriated when incriminating information was brought up. Many relentlessly defended Clinton, ignoring all evidence of wrongdoing. In all seriousness, I honestly wonder which would make some of these people angrier: Clinton losing his job or they themselves getting fired. They were probably as upset when Tripp provided proof of the Lewinsky affair as they would be if she divulged their own spouses' infidelity. This blind devotion to Clinton is an enigma to me. No doubt other young people found themselves facing this same quandary.

Linda Tripp Defamation

Once Linda Tripp tape recorded conversations with Monica Lewinsky in which Lewinsky discussed her relationship with President Clinton, she became prime meat for the Clinton attack dogs. These tapes played an essential part in exposing the truth. She informed the public about the president's immoral and possibly illegal behavior, and in doing so she risked everything.

In past instances uncovering corruption was viewed as a courageous action, telling the truth about the Democrat Clinton was another matter. As soon as the White House learned that Tripp had information, a full-fledged effort ensued to quiet her. When Michael Isikoff of <u>Newsweek</u> wrote a story on Willey, Tripp was told "'(Talking to Isikoff) is a dangerous thing to do.'" Tripp was warned "' You have two children to think about'" and talking "'is not a good career move'" (Snow, "Tripp: 'Fear is a magnificent motivator'"). Top aide Bruce Lindsey told Tripp that she would be "'destroyed'" if she talked (Snow, "Tripp: 'Fear is a magnificent motivator'")

Tripp knew the threats were real and the White House meant business. Tripp knew what happened to Billy Dale. He did not harm the Clintons, but was just in the wrong place at the wrong time. If the Clinton White House was willing to so vigorously pursue Dale, who just got in the way, imagine the extent they would go when someone actually did something against their interests. Tripp would soon find out.

The threats temporarily worked and she reluctantly refused to speak. In limbo between talking and silence, she had to decide whether to continue her reticence and have the security of her federal job and the accompanying perks or get fed up enough to tell the American people the truth. Tripp did the right thing by going public (Snow, "Tripp: 'Fear is a magnificent motivator'"). For this she paid dearly.

Reporter, Jane Mayer of <u>The New Yorker</u> served the first of many blows against Tripp. Somehow Mayer discovered Tripp was arrested as a teenager. Mayer asked Assistant Secretary of Defense for Public Affairs Ken Bacon for Tripp's response to question 21, parts a and b on Form 398 relating to her job. This part dealt with arrests. Bacon told his deputy, Cliff Bernath, to find the answer (Nordlinger, Why Didn't Bacon Get Fried?).

The story was authorities had arrested Tripp for stealing $263 and a $600 watch, and she failed to report it on her security clearance form (Leen, "Defense Department Probes Report of Linda Tripp Arrest"). This new development meant trouble for Tripp. How could the public believe her now if she lied about her arrest years earlier? Lying on a security form could be illegal. If she lied on her form, maybe she fabricated her allegations about President Clinton. It looked like Tripp was done for, at least until the truth came out.

Tripp's Washington Attorney, James Moody, said that stolen items were put in Tripp's pocketbook and the authorities arrested her (Leen, "Defense Department Probes Report of Linda Tripp Arrest"). At her arraignment the judge dropped the charges due to her innocence. Moody said, "'Linda was told by the judge she was unconditionally discharged and this would never appear on her record'" ("Pentagon investigating whether Tripp lied about her background").

The Pentagon wrongfully released Tripp's information. They had no right to release Tripp's files. The Privacy Act prevents the government from releasing private information, such as the information Bacon and Bernath released. Former U.S Attorney Joseph DiGenova said, "'The Bacon thing is a facial and obvious violation of the Privacy Act. It is made for it'" (Nordlinger, Why Didn't Bacon Get Fried?'").

Bacon claimed he released the information on his own, but this does not make sense. According to a Defense Department veteran, that is unlikely because "'Everyone who comes into public affairs is told Privacy Act rules. You don't release someone's confidential information-- to anyone much less the media. This is Public Affairs 101. And Bacon is perpetrating a shameful lie. Any professional in the building will tell you the same thing'" (Nordlinger, Why Didn't Bacon Get Fried?'").

Why did Bacon act so negligently? Why did he risk his career to hurt Tripp? Bacon knew the law. Was there a guarantee he would avoid consequences? Bill Clinton, whom the release benefited, was one person through his surrogates who could have provided Bacon such assurance, since he controlled the Department of Justice. At the time of the release, Tripp was an enemy of the state for trying to hold President Clinton accountable. Clinton knew he lied about Lewinsky, so he wanted to conceal the truth. Discrediting the messenger of the story as in times past was one way to accomplish that goal, and he did just that.

The evidence implicated higher ups and discredited Bacon's claim that he innocently released the documents on his own. Pentagon records showed Bernath wanted Tripp's information for a meeting with Defense Secretary Cohen. ("Judicial Watch-Defense Secretary Implicated in Violation of Linda Tripp's Privacy Rights"). White House testimony further indicated evidence of its involvement when the public learned Deputy Press Secretary Joe Lockhart referred Mayer to the Defense Department ("New Evidence Links White House to Effort to Destroy Linda Tripp"). This was key because Bacon said he disseminated the information on his own, but this new revelation contradicted Bacon. How much influence did Clinton's deputy press secretary exert in the release? Why was Lockhart concerned about Tripp?

The White House punished Tripp further when it dismissed her. Attorney Michael Kohn blamed Clinton for the decision because the president decides which political appointees get fired (Associated Press, "Linda Tripp Fired From Pentagon Job"). Yet even after the government fired her, she was still harassed. According to Tripp, allegedly the Pentagon released more private information about her search for a new job, information the Privacy Act protects. The public learned she applied for a government job at the George Marshall Center, a think tank dealing with security. Pentagon officials allegedly leaked information about her job interview to a European edition of <u>Stars and Stripes</u>. The article stated Tripp would accept a lower position and a pay cut. Tripp sued the Pentagon alleging abuse of her rights, claiming the recent leak abashed her and attempted to thwart her employment chances ("Linda Tripp Suing Pentagon over leaks designed to 'sabotage' career").

The lack of public outrage after the first release of Tripp's files reiterated that making public private information was still an acceptable tactic. Not surprisingly the Pentagon did it again. This is another example of the president's spin machine aiming its gun at the messenger and deflecting attention from the message.

Clinton's allies attacked and threatened Linda Tripp without reprimand. They probably broke the law attempting to malign Tripp.

However, nothing came of this due to the concerted efforts of the Justice Department and the media to procure "justice" for Tripp, better known as revenge.

The Tripp files were not just about Tripp and Clinton but also about the integrity of our government. Every year millions of Americans fill out extensive documents for the government such as tax returns, employment forms, etc. They tell the government this private information trusting it will remain secret. When the Department of Defense released Tripp's files, it not only broke the law, it broke the faith. It essentially broke into the archives and lit a match to the U.S. Constitution. Of course the liberal front groups such as the ACLU were no where to be seen. No doubt their organizations will return as soon as a conservative administration tries to enforce the law.

TrooperGate Threats

Bill Clinton's sexual partners were not the only people who risked character assassinations after making allegations. The troopers who bravely came forward with information against Bill Clinton got the same treatment.

Trooper Patterson claimed Clinton ally, Captain Raymond L. "Buddy" Young sent him a handwritten note worrying about Patterson's health. Young admitted writing such a letter but indicated he was concerned with Patterson's cholesterol levels and was not trying to intimidate anyone. Young also called three troopers, including Perry claiming concern for his friends. Trooper Perry recalled Young knew he had hired a lawyer and planned to go public with information in a book. According to Perry, Young then said, "'This is not a threat, but I wanted you to know that your own actions could bring about dire consequences'" (Brock, "Living With the Clintons Bill's Arkansas bodyguards tell the story the press missed").

If Perry, Patterson, and Young were three random people, one would have to believe the honest concern of Young. However, these are not three random people. Perry and Patterson witnessed the real Bill Clinton. Furthermore, these were not the only attempts at intimidation nor were they the only troopers threatened. Is it a coincidence that all Clinton whistle-blowers received the same treatment? No! It is evidence of a deliberate machination to hide Clinton's inappropriate actions from the public. This could only be accomplished through more Clinton-inspired corrupt acts.

Young's intentions seemingly were not innocuous, but what motivated him to threaten Perry and Patterson? Perry and Patterson had damaging information on Clinton, not on Young. Young said he called on his own, not for the White House or for President Clinton, but this also does not make sense. How did Young know Perry and Patterson hired lawyers and planned to go public? The White House with all its pull and connections might have been able to find this out. How could some regular guy have been able to discover this and why would he want to? Young, a friend of President Clinton, allegedly threatened people who had information about Clinton. Could the chief law enforcer have played a role in a scheme to intimidate and suppress the truth?

Although Brock recanted much of his tale, it has been independently corroborated by others, including the principles. What caused this transformation is not clear? Possibly it is "The Power of Material Goods" discussed in Chapter 5. Remember liberals are preferred at fashionable cocktail parties where they get to schmooze with celebrities. Brock circa 1994 probably wasn't deemed worthy to park their gas-guzzling SUVs.

Trooper Brown, also received the president's wrath. When "Mr. Brown agreed to a Whitewater interview with ABC News, administration officials erroneously told ABC that state records showed he was a 'pathological lair' and had flunked a CIA background check" ("The Washington Time-Ex-Trooper Will Tell of Bribery Attempt"). After Brown publicized his allegations, Clinton's allies told The New York Daily News not to believe Brown because he murdered his mother. This of course was not true. Regardless, Kendall and Clinton told the same accusation to ABC

News when it interviewed Brown ("L.D. Brown Testifies About White House Intimidation").

Clinton knew that the facts were his enemy. If he could make people reluctant to talk, then he could save his career. Brown, Perry, and Patterson risked their jobs and their future to inform the public. If the public did believe them, it would have created another major problem for Clinton and maybe encouraged others to come forward. Once again, Clinton and his allies did not let this happen.

My parents lessons contradicted this approach. I always thought hurting people through intimidation would get me into trouble. I thought that by bullying I would lose others' reverence, trust, and confidence. I thought such a tactic would prevent me from being successful. Did my parents teach me outdated values? Did my parents fail to prepare me for today's competitive world?

EmailGate Threats

In any other White House not archiving controversial emails in accordance with the law, would have been a major scandal. In the Clinton White House, however, it was only half of the scandal known as EmailGate. The other part, equally as suspicious, involved the Clinton administration's alleged actions once the problem was noticed.

Betty Lambuth, a contract employee and project manager, discovered the email problem and reported it to her supervisor at the White House, Laura Crabtree. According to Lambuth, Crabtree understood the seriousness of the problem and informed Mark Lindsay, a Clinton political appointee. Crabtree allegedly told Lambuth that Lindsay said anyone speaking of the problem would lose her job, be arrested, and thrown in jail ("White House Threatens Contractors with Jail").

Crabtree's response disturbed Lambuth, so she decided to meet directly with Lindsay. When Lambuth met with Lindsay, Lindsay repeated Crabtree's comments. He allegedly told Lambuth any contractor bringing the problem to light would be fired and go to jail

("White House Threatens Contractors with Jail").

The email contractors received other threats too. All five email contractors recalled a meeting on June 15, 1998 where Lindsay and Crabtree told them not to tell other workers or their bosses about the missing email problem. Lindsay testified that he had no recollection of the meeting with the contractors. Three of the five contractors testified that at the meeting they were threatened with jail, if they talked. In response to a question from contractor Haas, Crabtree told him he would receive "'a jail cell with your name on it'" if he squealed (Sperry, "All the President's Scandals"). Contractor Betty Lambuth testified she recalled the threat. Contractors Sheryl Hall and Sandy Golas also remembered hearing about the threat. At another meeting with Lindsay, Steve Hawkins, the contractors' program manager, testified feeling intimidated (Sperry, "All the President's Scandals").

Kathleen Gallant, the Associate Director for the Information Systems and Technology Division of the Executive Office of the President's Office of Administration, testified corroborating the threats. She believed that Crabtree and Lindsay were capable of intimidation and that the contractors acted threatened. She also testified that Hawkins told her that Crabtree threatened the contractors ("New White House Whistle Blower Claims Intimidation").

Crabtree and Lindsay, typical of Clinton aides, both testified that they did not make threats, contradicting the testimony of numerous contractors (Sperry, "All the President's Scandals"). Of course the denial was standard operating procedure and totally what one would have expected. When two people say two opposite things, one person must be lying. When two people say two opposite things under oath, one has broken the law and should be held responsible. Ample evidence exists to establish a prima facie case that Lindsay and Crabtree made threats apparently to suppress evidence. This was another perfect time for the Justice Department to do its job and catch the bad guys, even if you know them and they work for your boss. Of course, the Department of Justice's ultimate boss is supposed to be the public. Nonetheless, Justice gave them a pass.

An aggressive investigation, indictment and trial would have been a step in the right direction, putting pressure on Lindsay to reveal why he allegedly threatened the contractors. After all, the threats did not benefit him. The emails possibly contained subpoenaed information on FileGate, ChinaGate, campaign finance violations, and Lewinsky. If the contractors told the truth, he may have committed obstruction of justice. So why did Lindsay risk jail to hide those emails? Lindsay did not have much to gain, but Lindsay's boss President Clinton did.

One may think that threats in the White House are absurd because one would expect more from the most prestigious residence in the world. On the other hand isn't this sounding more like business as usual: stonewalling, obfuscation, etc., etc. The White House was not complying with the laws related to archiving emails. Why wouldn't Crabtree want the problem to be known, so it could be fixed? Why did Crabtree want the problem to remain a secret?

The infamous WaterGate tapes contained an eighteen and one half minute gap that played a pivotal role in Nixon era history. In EmailGate hundreds of thousands of emails vanished which may have pertained to misuse of the FBI, obstruction of justice, and more. With WaterGate the media rightfully demanded an investigation to determine the truth, but with EmailGate the media was stoic. This allowed another misdeed to drift by with no indictments, no accountability, and no truth. So what else is new?

Patrick Knowlton's Intimidation

Patrick Knowlton was another victim of intimidation. For days a succession of strangers appeared in a coordinated, rapid manner outside his apartment. They did not speak, instead they would stare. According to experts, federal intelligence and federal investigative agencies use this technique to threaten and to destabilize with the purpose of impeaching testimony (Shannan, "'Failure of Public Trust'").

On October 26, 1995 Knowlton and his lady friend noticed the first stalker when a person walked towards them while "constantly staring directly at Plaintiff's face...One directed a fierce glare into plaintiffs eyes as he approached, and continued this uninterrupted glare as he walked past Plaintiff. After they passed, ONE stopped and continued to watch Plaintiff as he raised his left wrist to his mouth and spoke into his coat sleeve" ("Ft. Marcy Park Witness Patrick Knowlton Lawsuit").

Within five seconds someone else came and started glaring at him. Then twenty seconds after the second person, another person approached and glowered at Knowlton. After the first five stalkers had come and gone, Knowlton recognized this was a full-fledged intimidation effort and feared physical harm. Because of extreme fear for his life, he began to feel physically sick ("Ft. Marcy Park Witness Patrick Knowlton Lawsuit").

Later that day as Knowlton and his friend were walking southbound, a car slowly drove by and pulled up on the curb ahead of them. Someone emerged from the car and stared at them as they passed. The man then reached into the car, pulling out a telephone or walkie-talkie, but Knowlton feared the man was reaching for a gun. The stalking continued on Friday, October 27, 1995 and on Saturday, October 28, 1995. The stalking ceased for the next two days, but one more episode occurred on November 2, 1995. As Knowlton left the elevator of his apartment building, Knowlton noticed a man outside with his back to the building. This man followed Knowlton. After making eye contact with Knowlton, he reached into a bag. Knowlton thought the man was getting a gun ("Ft. Marcy Park Witness Patrick Knowlton Lawsuit").

Knowlton experienced other incidents of intimidation. More than a year before, on his way to the Vietnam Memorial in his cherished 1975 Peugeot, he noticed a car tailgating him. After Knowlton arrived at the Memorial, he pulled forward to parallel park, when this car took the space before he could back in. Knowlton took another space nearby. When Knowlton and his group were out of sight, a nearby limousine driver witnessed the driver from the other car bash the taillights, headlights, the grill, and the radiator of Knowlton's car causing $3,700 damage (Shannan,"'Failure of Public Trust'").

This book is about the Clintons and how they are awful role models, so why is Patrick Knowlton in the book? Knowlton, as the others in this chapter who were threatened, had one common link: information and allegations that may have been detrimental to Bill Clinton and his administration.

Knowlton did nothing wrong. He was just in the wrong place at the wrong time and paid for it dearly. On July 20, 1993 Knowlton was stuck in traffic and at around 4:30 in the afternoon pulled into Fort Marcy Park to go to the bathroom. That was the same day and same place that Vince Foster died or at least the place where authorities discovered his body. Knowlton claimed he noticed a car he believed did not belong to Foster. When the FBI interviewed Knowlton, the FBI did not like Knowlton's account, so agents allegedly changed his comments. After Knowlton realized this, he complained, leading to his subpoena (Shannan, "'Failure of Public Trust'").

The day Knowlton was issued a secret subpoena was coincidentally the day the stalking began ("Ft. Marcy Park Witness Patrick Knowlton Lawsuit"). Was it a deliberate attempt to keep him from talking and make him seem paranoid and nervous in order to detract from his credibility? The timing seemed suspicious. Even more coincidental, Knowlton's car was vandalized the evening before his second interview with FBI Special Agent Monroe (Shannan, "'Failure of Public Trust'").

Who could have known about the subpoena and his FBI interview? The subpoena was secret, so only the FBI and the Independent Counsel knew ("Ft. Marcy Park Witness Patrick Knowlton Lawsuit"). It all sounds unbelievable, but there is considerable evidence and corroboration for much of it. What to make of it all? I just don't know.

A straight line of wrongdoing seems to exist possibly leading right up to the Clinton White House. For a young person this idea is shattering. Maybe I am in a fantasy world to expect more of my government. I thought many young people at one time in their lives yearned to be president or involved in government service. I thought we looked up to those kinds of positions because of the integrity they represent and the ability to make a positive difference. I thought the office of the president should be something to aspire to.

The incidents, surrounding Knowlton and the others mentioned in my book, make me question my premises about right and wrong. I realize that what happened to Knowlton might have had nothing to do with government agencies or the White House. Then again, maybe it had everything to do with it.

It is difficult to know who arranged for the stalking of Knowlton, if in fact it occurred. It could have been anybody all the way up to the highest levels of government. The public never learned much about it. No attempt was made to squeeze the little fish, so any big fish easily swam away. This was probably not an accident. If the public learned more about the alleged plot to intimidate the witness in the Foster death, we might have learned more about the circumstances, officially ruled a suicide.

Summary

Growing up my dad told me about a car accident that a very good friend had when he was a teenager with a female driver. The accident was not the friend's fault, but when he got out of the car he unleashed a tirade at the young lady. He made obnoxious, derogatory remarks. Witnesses observed this callow behavior and reported it to the police. Due to the verbal attack, the witnesses and the police decided he had caused the accident. The police officers logically concluded he had wronged and was trying to intimidate the lady in order to get off the hook. In the end, he was exonerated since the accident was not his fault. But he came very close to being fined for an accident he was not responsible for because of his boorish behavior.

My dad told me this anecdote so I could learn from his friend's mistake. The moral is not to verbally attack since these tactics can make you look guilty. If I do something wrong, I should come clean and take responsibility for my actions. If innocent, I should defend myself against the accusation by dealing with the issue. My parents' teachings made sense.

However, Clinton used "personal destruction" to discredit and prevent whistle-blowers from coming forward. Unfortunately, the tactic worked.

People associated with the Clintons also intimidated those would be whistle-blowers. These people often had intimate knowledge of private government information that few could have known. Many unexplained coincidences occurred during Clinton's reign, such as Willey's cat or Knowlton's car.

"Think about what ELSE was going on in November 1997.-the depositions being given, the stories of the people around Bill Clinton people who are here one day-and dead or ruined the next-and ask yourself if it is surprising that so many people around him have refused to testify, left the country or just experienced major loss of 'memory' when questioned" (Mostert, "What WAS the "Message" Sent to Kathleen Willey via Car Vandalism, and an Executed Cat?").

My common sense dictates that the Clintons were involved, but that is just speculation. The purpose of this book is to compare the contrasting lessons, not to get the Clintons. Whoever did the intimidation did it with the intent of helping the Clintons escape punishment. The fact that this tactic worked is important here, not who orchestrated the actions.

The threats delayed investigations and caused key witnesses to "forget" their information or flee the country. Character assassinations and threats created Bill Clinton's presidency and allowed it to last for eight years with few negative repercussions. The obvious benefactor was Bill Clinton. Laws were broken, justice was obstructed, and privacy was disregarded. However, no serious attempt for the truth and accountability ensued. Yes, he was impeached, but even that disgrace didn't seem to stick. The proceedings were more like a sideshow. The fines he could pay off with a ten minute talk to the Ethics in Government seminar in Beijing.

Parents try to teach their children what is right, but Bill Clinton taught them the opposite. In between working forty hours a week, paying credit card bills, and filing taxes, a concerned parent hopefully has time to instill values in their children, such as taking responsibility and not resorting to "personal destruction." The child hears this lesson, but he sees the Clintons who are living the good life immersed in these tactics. The good life his parents are striving to achieve, but often never quite able to get ahead of the mortgage payment. The child begins to think that those tactics are acceptable and necessary to attain success. When in a bad situation, he does not do what he has heard, but what he has seen work: the Clintons' methods. That is where the child's aspirations end and reality begins.

The average citizen can not get away with this and will have "hell to pay" if he or she tries. Even the powerful mob can not get away with this kind of behavior indefinitely. When you hear about perjury, defamation and intimidation, you should think of the Gambino family, not the First Family. It seems Clinton brought those strategies to the White House for his own personal benefit, and through his Justice Department and media connections walked away unscathed.

Part Two Conclusion

In recent years, the entertainment industry has received major criticism for the production of violent movies, violent video games, and violent music. These may be concerns, but all three are not real. Although they are inappropriate, they are entertainment.

The argument against these forms of entertainment is their accessibility glamorizes violence. Kids watching this constant barrage, get used to violence. Eventually some will become desensitized by it and not see it as bad. Some will even adopt the violence as their way of life.

This same logic applies to politicians and especially to the Clintons. Like violent entertainment, the Clintons were everywhere with one drastic difference. Although the Clintons' lives were made for Hollywood, they are real. Bill Clinton was president for eight years and Hillary Clinton has her eyes on the prize now in New York. The Clintons are tangible, a gun in a video game is not, so I think the Clintons were more negative, and will have more of an effect on young people.

The Clinton actions contradicted much of what my parents taught me. I learned honesty. I learned integrity. I learned what is right.

The best story I can tell about how my parents brought me up happened on a vacation trip to Las Vegas when I was young, maybe about eleven years old. My parents and I were waiting to ask the clerk a question at the registration desk of the Flamingo Hotel. The man in front of us was doing something, and he dropped a bill. I saw it on the ground. No one else did. Neither my parents nor the man saw it fall. The man did not turn around; he had no idea. I waited a second and picked up the bill. I looked at the denomination and saw three zeros, and then gave it back to the man. One thousand dollars, wow, that could have bought many video games or, if invested in the right IPO, could have been worth a good penny today. Of course at the time I did not think of that and still do not regret my actions. That is how my parents brought me up. It's not the Clinton way but it's the right way.

That is a much different lesson from the lessons the Clintons espouse. It seemed the Clintons would never do the right thing unless they had to. They did whatever it took to fulfill their ambitions.

The Clintons followed a clear pattern. They wronged, covered up and concealed. Then they adamantly denied. They were consistently inconsistent and used whatever stratagem available to get themselves out of the current situation. They used their friends' reputations to spread their claims, true or false, often coupled with someone somewhere doing something that could be construed as witness tampering and a barrage of character attacks and intimidation. They did anything to eschew accountability. They did anything not to take personal responsibility.

Some children will be effected by violent video games, while others will be affected by the Clintons' approach to getting ahead and staying ahead. I believe what the Clintons did will have more of an effect because the Clintons are real. Most children can tell that a video game is not real life and ignore the violence they see. However, few children can pass off the effect of the Clintons as just a game.

While some adults made excuses for the Clintons, I as a kid, could see the clear configuration of wrongdoing. Other kids must have seen it too and some of these will become desensitized and use the often underhanded actions of the Clintons, which no responsible parent would condone.

The worst part about the Clintons is not just what they did, but that their strategy worked. If the Clintons were properly punished, investigated fairly, and held accountable for the wrongdoing, it would have not been as negative. Parents could have said to their children that is what happens when people do bad or that everyone's actions catch up with them, even the president's. That would have been all right because parents could have used Clinton as an example to show their children do right, play fair, and obey the laws, but that did not happen.

Some children will think because Clinton was able to evade punishment, they can too. These children may become immune to illegal, unethical, and immoral behavior, but will be in for a big surprise if they end up in a jail cell smaller than a college dorm room. Other children will understand that Clinton got away with things because the media and the Department of Justice played politics. However, some of those kids will still be detrimentally affected. They will have learned from the Clintons that immunity is possible. They will think they will be lucky like Clinton. They will think they are invincible, which is a partial cause of other teen problems such as drug use and drinking while driving (it will happen to the next guy not me). The law will eventually catch up with these kids too.

I believe the Clinton effect is a real problem that has affected real children. Recently there has been major attention drawn to cheaters. According to surveys, about half of college students acknowledge cheating while three quarters of high school students admitted they cheated at least once in the past year. One in four students admitted to minor violations such as working with others on assignments that teachers had said students should do alone. One student attempting to explain the abundance of cheating among students said, "'If Clinton can do it and get away with it, why can't we?'" (Sohn, "The young and the virtueless"). Recently 122 University of Virginia students got caught cheating and faced serious punishment. Clinton conveyed the message that cheating was acceptable and possible. However, as we see from UVA, Clinton could get away with it, but the average child can not.

Another effect that Clinton probably had on children involved sex. According to the Alan Guttmacher Institute, kids as young as twelve years old are engaging in oral sex. These children believe that because there is no penetration, oral sex is not sex (Woodman, "Are You Prepared For Puberty?"). Hmm. Where have we heard that before?

The two above examples demonstrate that Clinton influenced some kids. He taught them oral sex and cheating. Not the negative repercussions of either, but that they can be done. He taught them that there are no consequences even if you do get caught. The Clintons were in an untouchable status, but the children who decided to follow in their footsteps are not. Those kids will get punished, will get kicked out of school, will not graduate, and will possibly be scarred for life. Unfortunately for our children cheating and oral sex were not the worst lessons that Clinton taught.

The Clintons taught a specific modus operandi to the younger generation. Some of the more impressionable children will emulate it. However, every young person will be affected by the Clintons, even those like me who did not follow their way of life. The reason is simple; the Clintons set a horrible precedent for all politicians. Politicians will see what they can get away with and may try to take advantage of certain situations. Some politicians, when caught, will say it's no big deal because others (the Clintons) did it. Even mob leaders and drug kingpins will see the possibility of corruption and immunity in politics and might get on board. The possibilities are endless, but it is you and I who will have the democracy we cherish tarnished.

Part Three

Lessons Confirmed, Sort of

Introduction

Yes, it sounds surprising, but some lessons my parents and the Clintons' actions taught me were similar. My parents taught me the importance of friends and associates. They also taught me the role of luck. The Clintons teach similar lessons in those areas. However, even then they managed to put a negative spin on the lessons that differed from my parents' teachings. This negative spin further shows the corrupting nature of the Clintons' legacy on the nation's children.

Chapter 8
Who You Know, Not What You Know

Growing up in my home, I never saw a "do what I say, not what I do" attitude because my parents taught me about life by example. Their expectations and role were clear. I did not always want to hear what they had to say, but I knew not listening would be met with negative consequences sooner or later. This upbringing kept me away from the Clintons' dismal influence and taught me many lessons for success: hard work, ethics, life is not always fair, and networking and connections are important.

Two individuals may apply for a job. One might be a little better credentialed, but the other applicant might be a friend of the interviewer. In that case, my parents said the job most likely goes to the friend. My dad reinforced this with a story he told about his brief stint as Director of the Office of Emergency Medical Services for the State of Connecticut. My dad needed someone with expertise in telemetry. He went to the Assistant Commissioner who explained the cumbersome procedures for hiring. My dad was told there had to be advertisements, numerous interviews, and a lot of red tape. Months passed with nothing but lip service on his request. One day my dad came into work and saw a new guy sitting at a desk. The guy was not in telemetry. My dad had no need for him, and the requested position was still unfilled. The long arduous process that the Assistant Commissioner talked about was bypassed. The guy clearly knew someone.

With my parents' guidance I learned the importance of leaving a good impression and always doing my best. I was told life sometimes is not predictable and I could not anticipate who I might meet again or where I would likely end up. An example of this is my senior year guidance counselor at Staples High School. I had not had this counselor since my freshman year in school. However, my hard work left a lasting good impression on him, so he nominated me for two awards. He did not have to do this, but he revered my effort. Obviously having a mentor in a position to be helpful is important.

The lessons the Clintons teach corroborate this. The Clintons were good at networking. Bill Clinton has tremendous charisma causing people to like him and want to assist him. He adeptly made many connections helping him to become attorney general, governor, and president. His career would not have been possible without the help of those friends and associates who aided him along the way. Therefore, both my parents and the Clintons' actions taught the importance of connections for success. However, that ends the similarities. My parents and the Clintons saw different things in friends and associates.

I learned that I should associate with moral, ethical people. My parents did not want me to surround myself with unethical people who lacked integrity and respect for the law. They reasoned those people would not best influence me, worrying that associating with unsavory characters might cause me to act in a similar way or desensitize me to inappropriate actions. Even if their inappropriate behavior did not psychologically affect me, by association I could still get tainted. For example, a police officer might pull over a car my friends and I were traveling in. These friends might have committed an illegal act before I entered the car or might have something illegal on them unbeknownst to me. This could get me into trouble too, even though I did nothing wrong. These fictitious disreputable friends could have gotten into trouble for something and even though I was not at the scene, the authorities still might question and detain me. My parents' teachings: don't look for trouble by associating with dishonorable friends made sense to me.

Many of the Clintons' closest friends and acquaintances are not principled, ethical, law abiding citizens. Perhaps the Monica Lewinsky scandal delineates this the best. Bill Clinton was accused of having sex with someone half his age in the White House, lying under oath about the affair, obstructing justice, and abusing power. However, not one Clinton associate gave up their position of power to make a statement that the president's actions were unacceptable. Everyone put power over morals and the law.

Dan Lasater

Dan Lasater was an Arkansas friend of then Governor Clinton and Roger Clinton. Lasater has always helped the Clintons. He donated $16,000 to Clinton's campaign and encouraged his associates to do the same. Lasater also let Governor Clinton use his plane. Lasater told the FBI he gave Roger Clinton a job at the governor's request and gave Roger Clinton an $8,000 loan to pay off a cocaine debt (Morrison, "Who is Dan Lasater?"). Governor Clinton seemed to appreciate Lasater's friendship awarding his company a $30.2 million bond to improve the state police's communication system. The deal netted Lasater $750,000 in fees (Mostert, "George W Bush, When Did you Stop Beating Your Wife?").

Although Lasater had a lucrative connection, he lacked integrity and respect for the laws. Lasater provided cocaine to friends. He served ashtrays of cocaine at parties at his mansion and stocked the drug on his jet. He told the FBI he dealt cocaine on at least 180 occasions (Mostert, "George W Bush, When Did you Stop Beating Your Wife?"). Lasater's involvement with cocaine was well-known and allegedly even Clinton knew about his friend's involvement.

According to Trooper L.D. Brown   he informed Governor
Clinton about seeing drugs on flights from Mena Airport, Clinton
responded "'that's Lasater's deal'" (Morrison, "Who is Dan
Lasater?").

The law eventually caught up with Lasater. In 1986 Lasater was
arrested and convicted of social distribution of cocaine. Lasater went
to jail for six months and was eventually pardoned by Governor
Clinton (Morrison, "Who is Dan Lasater?").

Lasater was punished for his illegal actions. However, Clinton
did not suffer on account of the actions of his libertine friend. My
parents said associating with and having bad cohorts could get me
into trouble. This was not true for the Clintons. Not only was there no
rebuke for their choice of buddies, but they often reaped benefit from
the associations.

Webster Hubbell

Webster Hubbell was a friend of Bill Clinton and a former Rose
Law Firm partner of Hillary Clinton. Bill Clinton once referred to
him as his closest friend. Clinton appointed Hubbell as the temporary
Chief Justice of the Arkansas Supreme Court. When Clinton ran for
president, Hubbell acted as a spokesman answering questions about
the Clintons' business interests and personal finances. After Clinton
was elected, Hubbell worked as a senior transition official who
screened proposed top officials. When the presidency began, Clinton
named Hubbell Associate Attorney General (Labaton, "A Clinton
Friend Admits Mail Fraud and Tax Evasion").

Obviously Hubbell was close to the Clintons. He had influence
and power, but it seems he had a negative side. On December 6, 1994,
Hubbell admitted he bilked at least $394,000 from over a dozen
clients while at the Rose Law Firm. Hubbell's victims included the
Resolution Trust Corporation, the Federal Deposit Insurance
Corporation, and Tyson Foods Inc (Labaton, "A Clinton Friend
Admits Mail Fraud and Tax Evasion").

From 1989 to 1992, on more than 400 occasions, Hubbell

submitted bills to his law firm to disguise personal purchases. He made fake expense vouchers and increased the hours of work performed for clients to hide the theft. He also avoided paying taxes on the money. Hubbell pleaded guilty to two felony counts of mail fraud and tax evasion. For each count, Hubbell could have gone to jail for five years and been fined $250,000 (Labaton, "A Clinton Friend Admits Mail Fraud and Tax Evasion").

In the end, the plea bargain reduced the sentence to twenty-one months. By that time authorities realized that Hubbell had stolen $482,410 and owed the IRS $143,747 (Gerth, "Ex-Clinton Confidant Gets 21 months").

Webster Hubbell was a white collar crook. Should Bill Clinton, an intelligent man and a close friend of Hubbell, have suspected Hubbell's dishonesty? Nonetheless, Clinton's friend, Hubbell, being so dishonest causes me to wonder about Clinton's personality.

Clinton could have found Hubbell work in the private sector, instead Clinton appointed him to a top position in the Justice Department. Hubbell risked disgracing the Clinton White House, when the truth became known. Why did Clinton risk political damage to give Hubbell major power? I see two logical reasons. Hubbell, as a close Clinton friend, possibly witnessed his friends' wrongdoing, so the Clintons may have wanted to keep a close watch on him. Another possible motive is the Clintons had a certain partisan vision for their Justice Department and knew Hubbell's past behaviors made him a prime candidate. Just as if you're going to steal FBI files, you get Craig Livingstone to do it, not Mr. Integrity, so maybe Hubbell was the exact fit for the Clinton Justice Department.

The average parent would not want their child to have anything to do with a Webster Hubbell—type individual, but he seemed to be a perfect friend for the Governor of Arkansas and the President of the United States.

The McDougals

James McDougal and Bill Clinton became friendly in the late 1960s while working on Senator J. William Fullbright's campaign. In 1978 McDougal and his wife Susan McDougal bought the Whitewater Development with the Clintons. In 1982 McDougal purchased Madison Guaranty Savings & Loan, which federal regulators closed in 1989 due to an abundance of bad loans. His business cost taxpayers $60 million ("Friends & relationships").

The average citizen would stay away from a con man and certainly would not go into business with one. What draws Bill Clinton to such people? Why doesn't a smart man like Clinton understand that, at best, hanging around garbage makes him smell too, while, at worst, indicates his complicity?

After Feds shut down McDougal's company, they indicted him on fraud charges, relating to Madison. A jury acquitted him, but he would not be as fortunate with the next indictment ("Friends & relationships").

McDougal was later indicted and convicted on eighteen fraud and conspiracy charges. The indictment stemmed from evidence indicating McDougal, along with his wife and Governor Jim Guy Tucker, cheated McDougal's Madison Guaranty and the Small Business Administration to obtain $3 million in illegal loans. Allegations arose that Bill Clinton participated. At first McDougal refused to cooperate with the special prosecutor, but then he became "'sick and tired of lying for the fellow'" (Haddigan, "McDougal Gets 3-Year Term"). McDougal began to cooperate, reducing the possible eighty-four year sentence he faced in jail to three years in prison, three years probation, $4.2 million in compensatory damages, and a $10,000 fine (Haddigan, "McDougal Gets 3-Year Term").

McDougal had much to tell but never had the opportunity to share. The day before McDougal died he was dizzy, breathless and vomiting in his jail cell, but he did not receive medical attention ("Report: McDougal had no access to heart drug, doctors just before death"). If McDougal received proper medical treatment, he might have survived. Unfortunately, we'll never know what he might have said.

However, we do know McDougal was a crook. He violated criminal laws and was the type of person my parents said to stay away from, but McDougal was the type of person Bill Clinton had no problem associating with. The same can be said about McDougal's wife.

Prosecutors indicted Susan McDougal for her participation in obtaining a $300,000 small business loan. A jury convicted her on four counts: mail fraud, misapplication of funds, making false statements, and false entries. She received two years in jail for the first three counts. For the fourth count the judge gave her three years probation, a $5,000 fine, and 300 hours of community service. She also had to pay $300,000 plus interest in restitution (Haddigan, "Susan McDougal Gets 2 Years for Fraud Tied to Whitewater").

Before she could even start her sentence for fraud, she went to jail for eighteen months for civil contempt because she refused to cooperate with the investigation. Her lack of cooperation caused Starr to indict her for two counts of criminal contempt and obstruction of justice. She refused to explain a note on a check, saying "'Payoff Clinton.'" She also refused to testify twice, although granted immunity. McDougal would neither answer Starr's questions nor those of the jurors (Schmidt, "McDougal Indicted for Silence on Whitewater"). A jury eventually acquitted her on the obstruction of justice charges and the jury deadlocked on the contempt charges (Werner, "Won't Retry McDougal on contempt counts, Starr says").

The McDougal friendship was not detrimental to the Clintons, but actually helped them. If the McDougals did the honorable thing, odds are the Clintons would have been in serious trouble. Susan McDougal, rather than staying silent, would have cooperated with the authorities. She would have told all she knew about the Clintons' apparent wrongdoing in Whitewater and Castle Grande. If James McDougal had integrity rather than "'lying for the fellow'" (Bill Clinton), McDougal would have revealed everything he knew and the public could have gotten his plenary account before he died. As the proverb says, "birds of a feather flock together."

Governor Jim Guy Tucker

Tucker, Clinton's lieutenant governor of Arkansas, became governor when Clinton resigned to become president. Prosecutors indicted Tucker along with the McDougals for his part in the illegal loan scheme related to Whitewater. A jury convicted Tucker on one count of conspiracy and one count of mail fraud, which involved a $150,000 loan to Tucker for the Castle Sewer and Water Company. For Tucker's illegal behavior he faced ten years in jail and a $500,000 fine ("Jim Guy Tucker, James McDougal-Guilty of Fraud and Conspiracy").

Tucker, Clinton's protégé, would have gone to jail if it weren't for his ill health. The judge was sensitive to Tucker's condition and rather than jail, put Tucker on probation for four years, placed him under home detention for the first eighteen months, fined him $25,000, and ordered him to pay $294,000 plus interest in remuneration (Haddigan, "Tucker Sentenced to 4 Years' Probation").

Tucker is another Clinton friend who broke the law. Numbers don't lie. If Tucker was Clinton's only convicted friend, one could easily assume Tucker's character duped Clinton. No one is perfect, not even a Rhodes Scholar. However, as the list gets longer, it gets harder and harder to rationalize that Clinton did not know what type of people his friends were. Remember, of course, in many of these transactions Clinton also was intimately involved.

Yes, the President of the United States does have a myriad of friends and associates, but Tucker did not hold an obscure, powerless position under Clinton in Arkansas. Tucker was his number two man in Arkansas. My parents said associating with dishonest people would reflect poorly on me. However, associating with criminals had no known negative effects on the Clintons.

Charlie Trie

Yah Lin, better known as Charlie Trie, moved to the United States in the early 1970's and eventually wound up living in Little Rock. He purchased several Chinese restaurants including the Fu Lin Restaurant, Governor Clinton's favorite. Through the business, the two became friends. In 1991 Trie started his own company, Daihatsu International Trading Co. In April 1996 Clinton appointed Trie to the White House Commission on Pacific Trade and Investment, a group of people studying U.S trade. Trie and his wife traveled frequently to Beijing, where they owned a house and a restaurant. In Washington Trie used his apartment to host many businessmen from Taiwan and China (Suro, "Indictment Secured In Fund Probe").

From his meager childhood, Trie had grown economically and powerfully, but his morals and ethics did not keep up. On January 28,1998 a federal grand jury indicted Trie on fundraising improprieties, accusing Trie of collecting money from foreign businessmen who were not allowed to donate to U.S. political campaigns. He then doled the money to U.S. citizens in order to funnel the funds to Democratic Party committees and the Presidential Legal Defense Fund. In 1996 when the investigation into his activities began, Trie fled the country (Suro, "Indictment Secured In Fund Probe").

Trie eventually returned to the country and pleaded guilty to one felony and one misdemeanor violation of federal campaign finance laws. Trie admitted to causing the submission of a false report to the Federal Election Committee stating that one individual had donated money when Trie knew another had. Trie also admitted to making contributions using someone else's name. For the two crimes Trie faced six years in jail and a $350,000 fine ("Charlie Trie Pleads Guilty to Federal Campaign Finance Violations"). Although Trie faced punishment for his serious crime, Justice only gave him a slap on the wrist: three years probation (Burton, "Opening Statement Chairman Dan Burton Committee on Government Reform").

Trie not only broke campaign laws, but he also disrespected our judicial system. Judicial Watch subpoenaed documents from Trie that he refused to turn over. Judicial Watch recommended that Trie be held in contempt for his reluctance ("Charlie Trie Recommended for Contempt in Judicial Watch Case").

Trie lacked the integrity my parents thought friends should have. Odds are most parents warn their children about the friends they choose. Perhaps even Bill Clinton's mom advised the same. No matter, look where he ended up. In fact, this corrupt friend's money raising helped Clinton's successful reelection bid. It is only logical for some children to dismiss the parental lesson and follow Clinton's example. Who knows, a child may even think if his or her parents had friends raising illegal money for them, they would achieve greater success. Just one small problem: the law.

James Riady

James Riady is a Clinton friend whose wealthy, powerful family owns the Indonesian conglomerate, the Lippo Group. During the Clinton presidency, Riady visited the White House numerous times. Materially, Riady had a lot, but he lacked the most important things: integrity, respect for the laws, and honor.

Riady entered into a plea agreement surrendering to American authorities and plead guilty to a felony charge of colluding to defraud the United States by reimbursing political donors with foreign corporate funds. His actions broke federal election laws. Between May 1990 and June 1994, Riady along with John Huang secretly indemnified contributions with money from prohibited sources. The reimbursements were carried out in several different ways. From May 1990 to July 1991, the foreign Lippo Group reimbursed donations that Huang and other LippoBank employees made. From August 1992 to October 1992, after Riady allegedly pledged a million dollars to President Clinton's campaign, Riady reimbursed Huang for contributions he made. The elaborate, illegal scheme was designed to benefit Riady's Lippo Group and LippoBank, giving them access to U.S. government officials in order to receive favorable government policies along with more business opportunities ("James Riady Pleads Guilty Will Pay Largest Fine in Campaign Finance History For Violating Federal Election Law").

Riady would have gone to jail for a long time, but because he is an Indonesian citizen, he avoided jail. U.S. authorities lacked the jurisdiction to forcibly extradite Riady to the United States. Riady returned voluntarily, but under the condition he would not go to jail. For his illegal contributions, Riady agreed to an $8.6 million fine, two years probation, and 400 hours of community service (Whitcomb, "Clinton Friend Riady Pleads Guilty, Fined $8.6 Million).

James Riady is another Clinton friend whose illegal actions benefited Bill Clinton. The illicit money that Riady and others gave was key to obliterating Senator Dole's presidential campaign before it had a chance to begin. The connection seems obvious. Of course the media missed it and the Justice Department did its best to hide it, but nothing new there. By intentionally giving wrongdoers these sweetheart deals, the Justice Department surrendered the opportunity to bargain away long term jail time in exchange for information implicating higher ups in these scandals. Justice followed a see no evil, hear no evil, prosecute no evil policy.

Johnny Chung

Chung was another corrupt acquaintance of the Clintons. He visited the Clinton White House on at least forty-nine occasions. Although the National Security Council identified Chung as a "'hustler,'" the Clinton White House gave Chung incredible access. Chung was not only a "'hustler,'" but would also soon be a convict ("Campaign Finance Key Player: Johnny Chung").

Chung pleaded guilty to illegally funneling $20,000 to the Clinton-Gore reelection campaign. Chung sought people to donate money to the campaign and then reimbursed them. Chung also pleaded guilty to charges involving an $8,000 contribution he made to the campaign of Senator John Kerry of Massachusetts, tax evasion, and fraudulently obtaining a loan on his home. For the four crimes the Clinton associate, faced thirty-seven years in prison and a

$1.45 million fine (Associated Press, "Democratic fund-raiser pleads guilty"). Chung, however, cooperated with the authorities and received a milder sentence of five years probation and 3,000 hours of community service (Associated Press, "Chung sentenced for illegal contributions").

If you needed money, would you accept ill-gotten money? I do not think so. It seems the Clintons did. The Clintons' association with shady friends was bad enough, but worse was that some of their suspicious actions benefited the Clintons directly. This yields speculation on the Clintons' involvement and the reason the Clintons befriended such people. A connection seems obvious. Yet, nothing ever came of it, meaning my parents were wrong again, I suppose. According to them, bad friends would make me look guilty by association. The Clintons suffered no punishment or even embarrassment by these friends. If anything, they profited. A regular mutual benefit association, you wash my back, and I will wash yours! This teaches my generation it does not matter who you associate with or become friends with. It does not matter whether your friends break laws, lie, or do other acts of wrongdoing—especially if there is something in it for you.

Jorge Cabrera

In November 1995, Cabrera donated $20,000 to the Democratic National Committee. Two weeks after the donation, Cabrera met Gore at a Miami fundraiser. Then ten days later Cabrera attended a White House Christmas function that Mrs. Clinton hosted. Cabrera had pictures taken with both Gore and Hillary Clinton (Van Natta, "Drug Smuggler Made Clinton Donation in Cuba, Investigators say").

If Cabrera could give $20,000 away, he must have been financially secure. The gift gave him access to power. Cabrera like all other Clinton friends, had much going for him, but had the same flaw as so many of the others, disrespect for the law.

An investigator requesting anonymity said that the account used for the donation included profits from cocaine smuggling. In January 1996, just three weeks after the White House Christmas gathering, authorities arrested Cabrea and charged him with importing 6,000 pounds of cocaine into the United States. He pleaded guilty to the charge. A judge sentenced him to jail for nineteen years and fined him $1.5 million. This was not Cabrera's first run in with the law. In the 1980's he was twice arrested for drug charges but pleaded guilty to nondrug felonies. In 1983 Cabrera served forty-two months in jail for bribing a grand jury witness. In 1988 he admitted to filing a false income tax return and went to jail for a year. (Van Natta, "Drug Smuggler Made Clinton Donation in Cuba, Investigators say").

Cabrera was a drug dealer. Although arrested twice, the Clinton administration still granted him access. Doesn't the Secret Service or the FBI do background checks on everyone entering the White House to ensure the safety of the president? How could this man have been allowed near President Clinton? If Cabrera was the only criminal friend of the Clintons, honest oversight was possible, or "whatever," but as we know Cabrera was one of a number of Clinton criminal associates. For any other administration, inviting a known drug dealer into the White House would have been a serious and devastating scandal, but for the Clinton White House it was just another day at the beach. Funny how you and I never got an invite.

Henry Cisneros

On December 11, 1997 a federal grand jury issued an eighteen count indictment against Cisneros, Clinton's former Secretary of the Department of Housing and Urban Development. Prosecutors accused him of conspiracy, obstruction of justice, and lying to the FBI. The indictment stemmed from evidence Cisneros attempted to hide the true extent of his relationship with his mistress, Linda Jones, and the amount of money he paid her. He told the FBI that the largest sum he gave her was $2,500 and he had not seriously talked with her since 1991. However, it seems both statements were not true. The grand jury accused Cisneros of talking to her after meeting with both the FBI and Clinton transition representatives. Cisneros also minimized the amount of money he gave her. According to the grand jury, Cisneros gave her several payments of $15,000 and paid her while still Secretary of HUD. In 1993 he gave her $73,000 (Locy, "Ex-Housing Chief Cisneros Indicted").

In the end, Cisneros pleaded guilty to one misdemeanor charge of lying to the FBI about the money he gave to his mistress, which resulted in a $10,000 fine (Miller, "Cisneros Pleads Guilty to Lying to FBI Agents"). I guess some people do get arrested for lying about sex.

Having an affair and brushing the law aside to cover it up, sounds quite familiar. No wonder Clinton nominated Cisneros for HUD, you know "birds of a feather…" Cisneros deliberately, in Clintonesque fashion, attempted to evade responsibility for his actions. Cisneros feared the truth might prevent his confirmation as Secretary of HUD, so he lied to the FBI. Cisneros' actions were unacceptable, but Cisneros was just another Clinton associate who should be written about in the "Who's Who of Big Shots Trying To Skirt The Law."

Terry McAuliffe

In 1993 Clinton nominated McAuliffe as an Ambassador and Commissioner General to the International Exposition in Korea. McAuliffe was the National Finance Chairman for Clinton-Gore '96 and was the National Co-Chairmen of Clinton-Gore '96. In 2000 McAuliffe chaired the Democratic National Convention in Los Angeles and became DNC National Chair ("Terry McAuliffe DNC National Chair").

Terry McAuliffe is another Clinton friend. As a young person reading about him, like the other friends I mention, it is better than seeing any action movie. There is the power, the money, the intrigue, the alleged illicit activity, and then the irony: I'm reading about real people; real people who rub elbows with the real President of the United States.

A scheme was plotted to secure a victory for Ron Carey as

president of the Teamsters over Jimmy Hoffa. Contributions to Carey's campaign were allegedly laundered through the DNC. Donors were persuaded to contribute to Carey on the condition that the Teamsters would indemnify the DNC with equal donations. Allegations existed that Bill Clinton's close friend and money man, Terry McAuliffe, actively participated in the plot. Four Democratic Party officials and Carey campaign workers implicated McAuliffe under oath, claiming he helped launder money ("Time For Him to Go").

Carey was removed as head of the Teamsters but the aforementioned prosecution fell apart for reasons that smelled of politics. The point is, doesn't the guy have any friends you could bring home to meet your mom? President Clinton seems to connect with those at the bottom of the honor code. I know I would not be permitted to "hang out" with the Clinton's cast of characters. I would have gotten grounded.

Ron Brown

Ron Brown was the Chairman of the Democratic Party and Clinton's Commerce Secretary. Brown was initially seen as a "'rising star'" of the Clinton administration. However, Brown quickly found himself under investigation. Allegations surfaced about bribery, causing a federal grand jury to be impaneled ("Nolanda Hill on Her Relationship With Ron Brown"). Unfortunately, we will never know the truth as he died tragically in a plane crash with rumors of an imminent indictment pending.

Secretary Brown did not make enough money to support his lifestyle. Nolanda Hill, an owner of two television stations, was a close friend of Brown. According to Hill, Brown received an offer from Vietnam emissaries. They would pay Brown if he lifted American trade restrictions. Brown allegedly contemplated the offer, but nothing ever happened because he learned that the FBI knew about the offer. Although the Vietnam deal failed, Hill claimed Brown received money from the Lum family, major Democratic contributors and owners of an Oklahoma gas company called Dynamic Energy Resources that sought government contracts. The Lums allegedly hired Ron Brown's son, as a way to siphon money to the father ("Nolanda Hill on Her Relationship With Ron Brown").

The most suspicious of Brown's activities were the trade missions, allegedly sold in exchange for donations. Hill claimed that Brown showed her a one inch thick packet of Commerce Department letters connecting the trade missions to contributions. Brown allegedly asked Hill if she thought he should destroy the documents. Brown had allegedly told her that the trips were being offered in exchange for contributions to the Democratic Party and the 1996 Clinton reelection bid (Associated Press, "Witness: White House sold trips for funds").

This raises speculation about the involvement of the Clintons. If true, why would Ron Brown sell the trade missions? The money did not benefit him. Why would he risk disgrace or worse for bribery or illegal fund-raising to raise money for the Clinton campaign? I can't understand why Brown would do that unless it was simply in the line of duty.

Hill alleged that Brown told her the White House organized the trade missions and that aides Leon Panetta and John Podesta told Brown not to cooperate with the court ("Witness: White House sold trips for funds"). These webs of intrigue go on and on and... maybe I'm just getting carried away. Maybe the trips were Brown's own idea and were strictly on the up and up. I don't know. I do know the search for the truth was terminated with the April 3, 1996 accident and won't be reappearing anytime soon.

Mike Espy

Mike Espy was a Congressman from Mississippi and Bill Clinton's first Agriculture Secretary. A federal grand jury indicted Espy on thirty-nine counts of illegally accepting gifts, while a member of the Cabinet, and covering up his activities. The charges alleged that he accepted over $35,000 in gifts, trips, and favors from businesses while head of the Agriculture Department. The grand jury also charged him with lying to prosecutors and ordering an employee to doctor a document. Most of the gifts came from companies he regulated. He faced a sentence of over one hundred years in prison ("Former Agriculture Secretary Espy Indicted").

Although the jury ruled that Espy was innocent of all charges, it was not in dispute that he received thousands of dollars in kind from companies he was supposed to regulate ("Espy innocent of all charges"). Senators must report gifts over fifty dollars from any individual. Espy took approximately seven hundred times that from companies under his jurisdiction. Even though the jury ruled him not guilty, I disagree with the ethics. It is impossible to be objective when one regulated company pays and another does not.

The jury spoke and I must respect their opinion. Espy may not have technically violated any laws, but one sure can question his judgment. He should not have taken gifts because they could inadvertently influence him and that is not right. For example, my dad refused to buy pharmaceutical and cigarette stocks when he was a practicing physician because it could give the appearance of a conflict of interest.

Although Espy was not convicted of breaking any laws, this was a type of situation my folks cautioned me to avoid. Of course on the Clinton scale this guy probably was rated "A" number one. After all, he didn't go to jail, didn't have to cop a plea, he even beat the rap. So what's the problem? Surely, Clinton could have found a qualified Secretary of Agriculture who would have held himself or herself to higher ethical standards, if that was a priority.

Don Tyson

Don Tyson, the Chairman of Tyson Foods, was a close friend of Bill Clinton. Tyson's company admitted to giving Agriculture Secretary Mike Espy $12,000 in illegal gifts, including football tickets, airline trips, meals, and scholarship money for Espy's girlfriend (Schmidt, "Tyson Foods Admits Illegal Gifts to Espy").

In the plea agreement Don Tyson and his son were granted immunity, but the company had to agree to pay a total of S6 million, $4 million for fines and $2 million for the cost of the investigation. At the time Tyson Foods gave these gifts to Espy, it was lobbying the USDA to slow the installment of meat and poultry handling instructions. The immediate effect of the rule would have cost Tyson Foods over $30 million (Schmidt, "Tyson Foods Admits Illegal Gifts to Espy").

Tyson, as head of his company, gave illegal gifts. Why did Clinton befriend someone like this and by all accounts remain good friends afterward? I always had to answer questions about my friends: what kinds of grades, parents, sports, their friends, etc. My parents wanted to know everything about my friends to prevent guilt by association, negative repercussions, and to insure that I would not get sucked into activities they didn't approve. My parents talked to me about society's pressures. If you are a parent or grandparent, I imagine you worry about your children: their friends, what they read, what music they hear, what they watch on television and in the movies. How come you found nothing wrong with the Clintons and their influence on kids? Parents, I know you read literature in order to be good parents. I see the books by Dr. T. Berry Brazelton on parenting, <u>Parents</u> magazines in your homes, what do they say about consistency? The parenting literature says consistency helps teach kids how to act. Consistently, kids saw the Clintons and these kids heard, read, saw the kinds of friends the Clintons had. Friends you probably would not want for your kid. Yes, parents you can rationalize that all presidents have skeletons in the closet, but this time they weren't in the closet. We, kids, knew about his friends, his lying, and his taking advantage of women. Did we learn from it? Unfortunately, of course, we did. The president is a role model. We also may think we can get away with it, after all he did. Many may forget or not know that the Clintons had media cover and the Justice Department to protect them. Will we get the same?

HOW TO DESTROY A VILLAGE:
WHAT THE CLINTONS TAUGHT A SEVENTEEN YEAR OLD

Summary

It is an irrefutable fact that the Clintons had some corrupt friends and associates. The Clintons' prior knowledge of their friends' malfeasance and the Clintons' involvement is not so clear. It is hard to imagine how the Clintons could have befriended so many shady people without knowing. A cynic might say they got exactly the people they wanted. Is it just a coincidence that so many of those friends' illegal actions benefited the Clintons? There may be no smoking guns, but it does seem strange.

However, for our purposes the Clintons' complicity does not matter. Parents tell their children the significance of good friends. These same parents knew the type of people Bill Clinton associated with when they voted for him in 1992 and certainly when they voted to reelect him in 1996. We saw them and their lawyers go in and out of courtrooms almost every day. These parents warned their kids about the negative effects of bad friends, but had no problem voting for someone whose closest friends and associates were consistently living on the edge and sometimes over it. Parents paid lip service to values, but refused to back it up on Election Day.

Parents can talk all they want, but kids learn by actions. The conflicting lessons probably leave children confused and frustrated. Why should any kid listen to a parent when that parent does not corroborate his words with deeds?

A Clinton sympathizer might argue some of Clinton's friends did break a law or two here and there, but they were not violent criminals. It is true, none of the previously mentioned Clinton buddies are murderers or even burglars, or-----I almost said rapist but in deference to the president I left it out. Besides there is nothing warm and fuzzy about white collar crime.

Chapter 9
One Hand Washes the Other

My parents taught me that I should always go out of my way to respect and help people. They said I should do this gesture out of the kindness of my heart. Furthermore, my parents felt one hand washes the other. By this they meant sometimes one who gives help may find the positions reversed in the future: what goes around, comes around. However, my parents said that if I tried to help a person who was unappreciative, not to worry about it. I should not be nice for rewards. Helping others is the right thing to do irrespective.

The Clintons had one hand washes the other relationships. However, I don't believe altruism motivated the Clintons. To me it appears, many of their actions were self-serving or designed to evade punishment. Many of the Clintons' arrangements seemed more like sleazy, under-the-table understandings involving a quid pro quo. Not exactly what my parents had in mind. Surprisingly, it worked for them.

Hubbell: Was It Hush Money?

After a criminal investigation forced Hubbell to resign from the

Department of Justice, the Clinton administration and its friends raised a substantial amount of money for Hubbell ("Clinton lied to White House Lawyers about Hubbell"). Hubbell made a plea agreement promising cooperation with the investigation in exchange for a lighter sentence. This looked bad for the Clintons. According to James McDougal, Hubbell knew everything. He was the man who "'knows where the bodies are buried'" ("James McDougal on CNN's Larry King Live").

The plea agreement reduced Hubbell's jail sentence, but he was still going to jail. If Hubbell helped the investigation, however, Starr could have further reduced his sentence (Gerth, "Ex-Clinton Confidant Gets 21 months").

Pressure mounted for Hubbell to talk. If he did, he could spend more time with his family and less time in a dark, lonely cell. Hubbell was not helpful. Thus, Starr refused to recommend a reduced sentence (Gerth, "Ex-Clinton Confidant Gets 21 months").

Hubbell did not provide the information, but he did give into a different pressure. He gave into the pressure of those associated with Bill Clinton and decided to "'roll over one more time'" ("Tapes: Hubbell Showed Concern About First Lady's Legal Work").

Just months after Hubbell resigned, he received numerous "'consulting fees'" that he did little or no work for. Clinton associates solicited over $700,000 (Schmidt, "Hubbell Got $700,000 for little or No Work, House Probe Says").

The Clinton-friendly, Riady controlled, Lippo Group gave Hubbell $100,000 for which little work was expected. President Clinton claimed ignorance, but this seemed unlikely. The week of the hiring, Riady met with both the administration and Webster Hubbell on numerous occasions (Tumulty, "The Hubbell Rescue Mission").

The Lippo Group was the first of many companies to help the disgraced Hubbell. McLarty solicited Truman Arnold, a friend of Bill Clinton, to grant "work" to Hubbell. Democratic donor Bernard Rapoport paid Hubbell $18,000 (Tumulty, "The Hubbell Rescue Mission"). U.S. Trade Representative Mickey Kantor and Vernon

Jordan, a close Clinton friend, also found Hubbell work. Clinton allies such as James Riady donated to three trust funds valued at over $110,000 organized for Hubbell to pay his legal bills, for his children's education, and living expenses. Competitors Sprint and Pacific Telesis Group Inc. both hired Hubbell, paying him a combined $112,000. HarperCollins also paid him over $60,000 for a book he never wrote. Democratic donor and Merrill Lynch executive Nicolas Stonnington even paid Hubbell $18,000 after his guilty plea (Schmidt, "Hubbell Got $700,000 for little or No Work, House Probe Says").

The Clintons of course admitted no wrongdoing and claimed that White House aides helped Hubbell as a friend. This lame excuse just does not hold up. For starters the Clintons have never admitted wrongdoing unless their backs were against the wall, as in a stained blue dress, so this denial is no surprise. The timing is suspicious. The money began to come to Hubbell after he resigned and was under investigation. To my knowledge it was not established he ever did any real work for all this cash.

From the time of his resignation to the time of his guilty plea, Hubbell met with White House officials, including the Clintons, over seventy times ("Clinton Lied to White House Lawyer about Hubbell"). It can be speculated at one of these meetings an off the record understanding was reached. Hubbell and his family would profit financially if he kept quiet. What is known for sure, he did not talk and the free money rolled in. One can only imagine Clinton's fate, if Hubbell had come clean with the information the special prosecutor believed he could provide.

Common sense further dictates more to the money exchange than the Clintons ever admitted. Hubbell had just left the Justice Department disgraced and was under investigation for fraud. No company would want to give a person a good job with that on his resumé. Why would such powerful important people push so hard to get "work" i.e., money, for the publicly humiliated and soon to be convicted Hubbell? Do these people really seem so philanthropically oriented? Remember, Clinton is the guy who took a deduction on his income tax for donating old underwear to charity. Furthermore, let us not forget Hubbell gets convicted for stealing money from his clients.

I think the Clintons orchestrated assistance to Hubbell for their own good as much as for him. It seems Hubbell's silence could be bought and the Clintons took advantage. In my opinion this was a matter of necessity not just friendship, not a demonstration of high-minded principles, rather it smacked of self-preservation and cover up. If that is what it took to keep Hubbell quiet, no problem!

Besides lacking altruism, the Clintons also seemed to lack integrity because the help covered up and concealed the truth. I was taught this kind of stuff was just plain wrong. Hubbell allegedly knew everything about the Clintons, but once he got that money he decided not to share.

Tucker Money

When Jim Guy Tucker, Clinton's lieutenant governor, got into legal trouble, Clinton friends helped him and his family. After Starr indicted Tucker in 1996, James Riady and Joe Giroir, Mrs. Clinton's former law partner, arranged a profitable deal for Tucker's wife, guaranteeing the family at least $325,000 a year. After Tucker was convicted and faced a lengthy prison sentence, Riady helped Tucker again by hiring him. Riady arranged the job after Starr announced Tucker's cooperation, possibly attempting to deter Tucker from talking about Clinton. The timing of the deals was suspicious to say the least (Morris, "Jim Guy's Hush Money").

When it looked like Tucker might go to jail, Riady and Giroir stepped in and provided money to his family. After the jury convicted Tucker and he faced jail, he received further help getting a job. The arrangements were suspicious. Most companies do not hire people recently indicted and convicted of fraud. This seemed strange, unless the job was based on silencing Tucker's information. Tucker was involved in a fraudulent conspiracy in which Bill and Hillary Clinton also allegedly took part. One could reasonably conclude that Tucker's honey pot was conditional on his lack of cooperation. The money put Tucker in a position where he had everything to gain by not talking. No there is no proof to back up these suspicions, but who hires disgraced former government officials at high pay for little work? Think about it. Notice the same group of benefactors keeps showing up to save the day.

Contrary to my parents' teachings of unconditional benevolence, the Clintons and their cadre appear to only help people when they can get something in return. While my parents taught me the idea of interdependence for the good of the whole or the "village," the Clintons represent personal gain. Nonetheless, this self-centered approach worked for the Clintons.

Lewinsky Job

Monica Lewinsky sought a job in New York since July 1997. Clinton agreed to help her, but did nothing. On November 5, 1997 Lewinsky met with Clinton friend, Vernon Jordan. Nothing came of the meeting. On December 6, 1997 Lewinsky reported to President Clinton that she did not have any luck with Jordan. Without a sense of expediency, Clinton said he would try to talk to him again. However, five days later it became exigent. Lewinsky met with Jordan on December 11, 1997 and he called three potential employers. Later that day Jordan called Clinton to inform him about the job search. On December 11, 1997 President Clinton went from apathy to extreme concern. The date was no accident. On that day Judge Susan Webber Wright gave Paula Jones the right to access information about state and federal employees with whom Clinton had or solicited sexual relations. That meant her lawyers could question Monica Lewinsky ("The Starr Report").

On January 7, 1998 Monica Lewinsky signed a false affidavit. She showed it to Jordan who had arranged a job interview for her with MacAndrews & Forbes in New York for the next day. After the interview Lewinsky called Jordan to tell him that the interview did not go well. Jordan then called the CEO Ron Perelman. That night the firm called her back and requested more interviews for the next day. After those interviews, the company offered her a job. When Jordan heard the news, he told President Clinton, "'Mission Accomplished'" ("The Starr Report").

The contacts between Clinton and Jordan regarding the search, indicated Jordan obtained a job for Lewinsky at Clinton's request ("The Starr Report"). Clinton was not looking out for the interests of Lewinsky. I don't think he cared about the future of his young mistress. He only helped her when she was in a position to help him. Clinton, for political and family reasons, did not want the relationship known. Thus, on December 11 when a judge said Lewinsky could be questioned in the Paula Jones case, Clinton became concerned about Lewinsky's job search. At that time he got Jordan to seriously help her. Once she signed the false affidavit, Jordan on behalf of Clinton got her the job. The job was apparently given to her in exchange for denying the relationship. At the time, her denial auspiciously allowed him to confidently deny the relationship publicly and under oath ("The Starr Report"). Clinton probably thought the Lewinsky affair was a case closed, and he had successfully thwarted Jones' lawyers. The Lewinsky dress and tapes made his victory ephemeral.

Clinton's actions, unlike my parent's lessons, show a selfish man who only cares about himself. People concerned with doing what's right, do what's good for the community ("village"). They put the interests of others before their own. Was Clinton's lying about this affair good for the people and Paula Jones, in particular? No, he did it for his own benefit. The attempt to silence Lewinsky was intended to circumvent the Jones lawyers' search for the truth and prevent Paula Jones from having a fair day in court.

McDougal Pardon

Many speculated about Susan McDougal's lack of cooperation in the Whitewater investigation. Her refusal to testify sent her to jail for eighteen months for civil contempt. Starr later indicted her for criminal contempt, but the jury could not reach a verdict. Although granted immunity, she would not testify. She blamed her lack of cooperation on Starr, but even when the jurors asked her questions directly, she still refused to talk. Susan McDougal's silence served a major blow to Starr's investigation and aided President Clinton. Could there have been an agreement with President Clinton? Would any of us go off to jail once granted immunity rather than answer questions honestly? What principle could she possibly be defending? It just does not figure.

Her reticence caused many people to raise the possibility that Clinton had bought it by promising a pardon (Levin, "The Clinton Clan"). Jim McDougal, the former husband of Susan McDougal, claimed during their trial President Clinton had promised her a pardon if they denied Clinton's involvement in Hale's $300,000 loan to Susan McDougal (Schmidt, "J. McDougal Book Says Clinton Lied Under Oath").

When television journalist Jim Lehrer asked Clinton about the rumors of a promised pardon, Clinton denied them. He had not thought about pardoning her, and besides her pardon would follow the normal process just like any other. Clinton said, "'there's a regular process for that, and I have regular meetings on that, and review those cases as they come up after there's an evaluation done by the Justice Department'" (Levin, "The Clinton Clan").

Well, that was a lie. A normal process does exist for pardons, but Clinton bypassed that process with the McDougal pardon. Susan McDougal's pardon was one of about forty the Justice Department did not examine (Levin, "The Clinton Clan"). Someone should remind Bill Clinton of his previous statement. His excuse might be interesting. Maybe one of the star network anchors could raise that question when they do their next puff piece interview with the former president.

Both sides won. McDougal got a pardon. Unlike others who gave significant money to Clinton relatives or Bill Clinton's presidential library coincident with a pardon, McDougal just had to refuse to cooperate and go to jail. Her slate was wiped clean. Clinton, on the other hand, benefited because another possible informant with inside information on an illicit loan, another affair, or who knows what else, did not talk. McDougal got a pardon and Clinton got silence.

The quid and the quo seemed obvious but was it an agreement designed to obstruct justice or did Clinton pardon her on the merits? My common sense supports an understanding between the parties, otherwise why would Susan McDougal have gone to jail rather than talk? She could have played hardball for awhile. However, once threatened with jail, she most likely would have talked. McDougal's silence got her into more trouble and put her in jail for a long time. If McDougal had not been holding out for a pardon, why would she have obstinately stayed silent?

If the pardon was based on the merits, and not a reward for her silence, why did Clinton not pardon her in the first term? Clinton was too shrewd to do that. If McDougal deserved a pardon, why did her pardon not go through the normal pardon procedures? This bypass seems to indicate Clinton knew no merits existed for the pardon.

President Clinton did not pardon McDougal out of the goodness of his heart or even as a token of friendship. He mostly helped those who helped him, and Susan McDougal certainly did that. I doubt there would have been a pardon in the cards for Jim McDougal, if he lived. This was not my parents' teaching, but again, it worked for Clinton.

Summary

I was brought up to be respectful and helpful. I learned that at an early age from my beloved Uncle Robert to whom this book is dedicated. Unfortunately he died while I was in the eighth grade of pancreatic cancer, but he left an indelible impression. He was an honorable man who always went out of his way to help everyone he could. Helping others is the right thing to do whether or not it benefits me personally. By being unselfish, I am encouraging others to treat me in kind. Thus, one hand does wash the other, in the context of the greater good. In this way, each person contributes to the good of the community or "village."

HOW TO DESTROY A VILLAGE:
WHAT THE CLINTONS TAUGHT A SEVENTEEN YEAR OLD

President Clinton did not eagerly help our "village," only himself. Most parents would not teach this narcissistic way of life. Most parents would not tell their kids to only hold the door open for someone if they are wearing a mink coat or expensive jewelry.

However, these same parents were responsible for giving Bill Clinton's self-centered behavior the green light. We live in a democracy. A mutual relationship exists between politicians and the people. The people elect politicians and the bottom line for them is to get reelected. This means that politicians rarely do something the overwhelming majority of the population opposes. If there had been a mass outcry, for example, when Hubbell got what sure looked like a pay off, Clinton probably might not have pardoned McDougal on the sly, or not done any number of things he got away with. However, these adults and parents were not incensed. Accordingly Clinton was free to do pretty much as he pleased and he did.

Parents would be upset if their children only called their grandparents around Christmas and their birthday in order to insure a present. However, when the country's putative role model did a similar stunt, these parents looked the other way.

What should a child do? What lessons will be taken away from all this? Parents warn against purely opportunistic behavior. They advise do the right thing without expecting something back. Clinton continually did the opposite in plain view. The tactics worked and many parents supported him anyway, no matter how self-centered, self-serving his actions. Any surprise here if kids reject the parents' teachings.

Kids learn best by the examples parents set. Parents can preach the significance of saving money until the cows come home but if they spend every penny on useless gizmos and gadgets, odds are their talk will not resonate with their children. The same is also true with cigarettes. Parents can tell their children about the health risks from tobacco, but it doesn't mean much if those parents are smokers themselves. Kids learn by actions. Why wouldn't it be the same with the Clintons? Parents overlooked his egocentric behavior at their kids' peril.

Chapter 10
Luck

My parents taught me that people could work hard and have all the connections in the world but still not succeed. These people lack one ingredient they can't control, luck. Sometimes one needs to be in the right place at the right time. One minute can make all the difference. If you are unlucky, terrible things can happen. For example, Patrick Knowlton could have gone to a fast food restaurant on the road instead of Fort Marcy Park to use the toilet. He could have left work twenty minutes later and gone to the bathroom in the park twenty minutes later and would not have seen a car other than Foster's in the parking lot. He went to the park when he did, saw the car parked there, and was later terrorized for speaking out. It was fate. Knowlton, like many others, had bad luck and paid dearly. The Clintons had a tremendous amount of luck and it allowed them to survive.

People made many charges against the Clintons. Suspicious patterns and connections existed among many of the allegations that could not be ignored, but the Clintons never were convicted or held accountable for any of these credible claims. This was due in part to luck. President Clinton eventually had to admit to two scandals because of irrefutable evidence supporting the allegations: a semen stained dress and the Gennifer Flowers' tapes. These were smoking guns and ultimately Clinton could do nothing about them. The scope of both scandals went well beyond extramarital relationships but that is all Clinton was forced to admit. One would think that a sexual affair would be unacceptable for a president or a presidential nominee. Not so for Clinton. He was lucky that the smoking guns didn't fire in another, more serious allegation. There could have been a memo of Clinton requesting an illegal loan. There could have been a tape of him ordering the intimidation of a potential witness. Many different kinds of evidence could have surfaced giving irrefutable proof of what now remains only alleged illegal involvements.

Clinton was also lucky because of his party affiliation. If Clinton had been a Republican, he would have never gotten away with what he did. The media played a pivotal role in protecting Clinton, which they never would have done for a Republican.

Clinton was also lucky because of the strong economy during his presidency. People may disagree over the roots of the economic success. The fact is that the economy was rebounding when Clinton ascended to the presidency and took off when the Republicans gained control of Congress in 1994. Others may think differently, but regardless, without the economic success, Clinton would have been toast. The increased stock market valuations and rising economy caused some people to turn the other check to his proclivities. People were satisfied with the pay check and opted to look the other way when it came to character issues.

This shows something about the electorate. The fact that adults let President Clinton get away with actions contradicting their advice quite possibly teaches my generation the worst lesson of all. Namely, that parents really don't care about morals or values. They don't care about honesty or doing the right thing. These parents care about success and money more than character. The support Clinton maintained through impeachment and their willingness to forgive and make excuses teaches kids parents really don't care about ethics.

Parents may pay lip service to it, but when push came to shove, their actions spoke louder than words. These parents did not practice what they preached, so why should any kid take parents and their preaching seriously?

Clinton was lucky. The strength of the economy no doubt helped keep him in office. This was good for him, but bad for our children. Children are more superficial than adults are. Children are easily attracted to money and power, so if the Clinton economy impressed adults, imagine how children were impressed with the president. The President of the United States is the most powerful man in the world and has unlimited earning power after his stay in the White House. Clinton had what many young people dream about, so many probably looked up to him and admired his way of life. They may conclude success may be theirs if they adopt the Clinton formula or more simply, if Clinton did it, it's just not wrong. Certainly those children who follow in Clinton's footsteps will meet a lesser fate. John Q. Citizen can not rely on the luck of a strong economy or a timely "suicide" to pull him through; that is why we need honorable leaders and avoid those who represent a lowered standard. There will be a price to pay for Clinton's luck. I fear it will be paid by society's children.

Part Three Conclusion

Some lessons on which the Clintons and my parents would have agreed were derogated by a certain taint the Clintons managed to spin into them. Their true colors always showed through. They just could not escape who they were nor in fairness did it appear they wanted to. They had a number of troubling friends. The Clintons did their best to help themselves first, usually before these associates were arrested but sometimes even after their convictions. Often assistance to an acquaintance was a double edged sword. It was only extended where there was possible advantage back to the Clintons. I can not recall a time in Clinton's very public career where there was a display of single minded generosity with absolutely no evidence of quid pro quo. Although my parents taught me ethics and altruism, the Clintons show a lack of both.

Maybe you are trusting and believe it was a bad apple here or a fluke event there. If it was just one appalling friend or one issue of alleged silence for sale, maybe that reasoning works. However, there was a pattern of wrongdoing. It was never just one. This simply can not be ignored. Perhaps if the media did more to support investigative bodies and pushed harder for answers, a la Nixon and Watergate, more stones would have been uncovered, more dots connected, and more answers forthcoming. It was not to be. Don't count on this accommodation if your child has stepped over the line. Unfortunately, there is no disclaimer to the Clinton presidency warning young people, who may have witnessed it: "Don't try this at home."

Bill and Hillary Clinton were everywhere during my childhood. They set less than exemplary standards. Luckily my parents had time and persistence to teach me correctly, so the Clintons did not sway me, but other children may not have been so fortunate. Other more impressionable children may have picked up on the Clintons' tactics and thought of incorporating those actions into their own lifestyles. Some may have seen the Clintons' success and thought that their machiavellian approach is necessary to succeed in today's society. Others may have used this as an excuse to justify their own wrongdoing.

Spinners and politicians can argue issues and defend allegations, but it would be difficult for any fair minded person to conclude the Clintons had a good effect on young people. He was a poor role model who escaped accountability, thus giving children the impression that associations with the wrong people and altruism are not important. Most parents would teach the exact opposite. It was not just luck that allowed Bill Clinton to emerge from the cauldron unscathed. He is obviously a very intelligent person and shrewd politician, but that does not absolve him. Escaping responsibility was the worst of all results. If Clinton had been seriously held accountable, parents could have used that to reinforce honesty and values. Parents could have taught kids how having bad associates can get even the president in trouble, so take care when choosing your friends. Clinton's luck held and this did not happen. Thus, children and adults will have to draw their own conclusions.

There is no question in my mind that the immunity of the Clintons planted seeds in the minds of some of my generation that unsavory things could be done without consequence. Let me slow down, because I might have been a little simplistic. More than luck and smarts saved the Clintons. Yes, he was lucky, but it wasn't luck that caused the Justice Department to feather his bed nor was it luck that the mainstream media often came to the rescue by blatantly pooh-poohing many of his scandals. It was agenda driven politics.

Part Four
The Difference

Introduction

The Clintons did not change me, but they did make me think. Who was right? Were my parents overzealous, overprotective parents and out of touch with today's world? Had society descended to a point where everyone acted like the Clintons? Perhaps they indeed were the standard, maybe even the gold standard.

After some thought I concluded my parents were right. Ethical, honest, and law-abiding traits can succeed without bending the rules. The Clintons were just an anomaly protected by two key forces the average citizen does not possess. Necessary elements that allowed the Clintons to prevail and without which imitators are doomed to fail.

The Clintons taught us kids that anything was possible. Even if you get caught stealing candy from a baby, you can avoid punishment. There will always be a way out. I have come to realize that was an illusion. Real people can not avoid accountability for inappropriate behavior. The media and the Clinton Justice Department refused to do their jobs. They protected the Clintons. They refused to aggressively seek the truth. They hoodwinked many adults into dismissing the allegations as partisan lies. They ran interference for the Clintons thus allowing them to escape responsibility. Don't count on them doing it for you.

There are ramifications for lying and penalties for perjury. For anyone else, a pattern of apparent wrongdoing would not indefinitely be ignored as happenstance. At some point the dots would start to connect and redress would ensue. My parents taught me a way of life that does not get one into trouble. They tried to warn me about the consequences inappropriate actions could have on my family, friends, job, and future. There was one unexpected curve ball, a president who contradicted their teachings.

At first I was ambivalent and confused until I realized the Clintons did not care about me. They only cared about themselves. The Clintons did not care what strings were pulled as long as they prevailed. Despite all their lip service to children's issues, they did not care one iota about the false lessons they spread, and the impact they would have.

Chapter 11
The No Justice Department

The Justice Department is one of the most important government agencies. It investigates and holds accountable those in violation of federal laws. It has significant power and should function independent of political influence to be effective and credible. Otherwise there is a grave risk of wrongdoing, corruption, and tormenting political opponents while looking the other way when someone deemed friendly is the target.

In my opinion the Reno Justice Department was thoroughly politicized and deserves much of the blame for Clinton's success in dodging the bullet and landing on his feet through the eight years of turmoil. Along with this dubious distinction she must accept a share of the consequences. Attorney General Reno's actions played a key role in contradicting parental teachings time and again making it look facile for Clinton to slip through the dragnet and evade responsibility for his misdeeds. It was not just incompetence, she was complicitous. For those kids who grew up believing they could outsmart the system, they better realize fast a Janet Reno is not in their hip pocket.

Donald Smaltz and Justice

Donald Smaltz was the independent counsel appointed to investigate Mike Espy. He started investigating gifts received by Mike Espy and then moved on to the gift givers, including Don Tyson. Smaltz hoped to find someone with knowledge of Tyson's relationship with Espy or whether Tyson gave gratuities to other public officials. Smaltz met with Tyson's ex-pilot, Joe Henrickson. Henrickson cooperated, but knew nothing about Espy. Henrickson did say that Tyson asked him to deliver envelopes containing one hundred dollar bills to then Governor Clinton (Boyer, "Secrets of an Independent Counsel").

Smaltz thought he had discovered a pattern of significant wrongdoing and requested authority to expand his investigation into other Tyson related activities. The expansion was a legitimate request, but surprisingly Attorney General Janet Reno refused. This decision closed the part of the investigation pertaining to Henrickson's allegation and other gifts Tyson gave, thereby limiting the focus to Espy. To Smaltz's knowledge the Justice Department did nothing to investigate the allegations Smaltz uncovered. "'I think it's buried,'" said Smaltz (Boyer, "Secrets of an Independent Counsel").

Smaltz did his job to investigate and search for the truth. Janet Reno did her job, as Clinton's chief protector. There was no legitimate reason for Reno's blocking the investigation. Janet Reno was supposed to carry out justice and punish those who broke the laws; yet, her decisions did the opposite. If Reno let Smaltz investigate Henrickson's claim, there is no telling what might have been uncovered. If true, Clinton might have been in big trouble. The attorney general's job is to find the truth wherever it leads, but all too often she preferred to slam the door when the trail approached her bosses' domicile.

Tyson was a close Clinton friend with intimate knowledge about his dealings. If Smaltz had investigated Tyson's dealings beyond the Espy matter, he might have uncovered significant wrongdoing on the part of Tyson and used the leverage of possible jail time to secure a plea deal and a cooperating witness. Who knows where that might have led? It seems Clinton and Reno did not want to risk that happening, so the investigation stopped before it had a chance to begin.

Michael Brown and Justice

The Justice Department gave Michael Brown, the son of former Commerce Secretary Ron Brown, a sweet deal. When Ron Brown died, the independent counsel had been investigating his practices and those of his son who allegedly acted as an intermediary for his father's bribes. The death terminated the Ron Brown investigation and the investigation into Michael Brown was turned over to the Justice Department. The Justice Department decided not to further investigate Michael Brown and reached a plea bargain based on the information available. In the agreement Michael Brown admitted to illegally funneling money into Senator Kennedy's reelection campaign. Brown gave $2,000 to the campaign and then got two other people to donate $2,000 who he later indemnified. Brown could have been charged with felonies, but the government only charged him with a misdemeanor (York, "Michael Brown Goes Free").

The Justice Department agreed to end the investigation into Brown's practices and freed Michael Brown from further punishment for the alleged payoffs. It completely ignored evidence that Michael Brown transferred bribes to his father (York, "Michael Brown Goes Free"). Nolanda Hill, Ron Brown's close friend, and Stuart Price of Dynamic Energy Corporation, both confirmed the company used Michael to pay Ron Brown ("Michael Brown Sentenced to Minor Violation of Campaign Finance law in Face of Evidence That He Was Conduit of Bribes to His Father, Former Clinton Cabinet Secretary Ron Brown").

The Justice Department helped Michael Brown. If the investigation had continued, he could have been indicted and convicted for more serious crimes. Ultimately Bill Clinton may have been the primary beneficiary of this deal. A continued investigation into Michael Brown might have linked the actions of his father, the Commerce Secretary, to the Clinton administration.

Nolanda Hill claimed Brown did the trade missions on orders from the White House and that the White House also ordered Brown to withhold documents. ("Witness: White House sold trips for funds"). If Michael Brown had faced a lengthy prison sentence, he might have come clean in return for a reduced sentence. The Justice Department's plea agreement, however, insured he got a slap on the wrist removing any incentive to cooperate. The Justice Department's plea "'effectively swe[pt] under the carpet not only serious violations of criminal law, but also effectively shut down and remove[d], the use of Michael Brown as a means to gain more information about the Clinton campaign finance and other scandals'" ("Michael Brown Sentenced to Minor Violation of Campaign Finance law in Face of Evidence That He Was Conduit of Bribes to His Father, Former Clinton Cabinet Secretary Ron Brown").

The Justice Department's job is to get to the bottom of issues and hold those people who are responsible, accountable for their actions. However, when an investigation or prosecution might have implicated the Clintons, the Justice Department seemed to do everything in its power to conceal the truth. If the investigation into Brown had continued, like the evidence called for, who knows what might have been learned about Michael Brown, his father, and the Clintons? Just one more example of the powerful protecting the powerful.

Tripp files and Justice

When the Pentagon released confidential information from Tripp's files, the Inspector General investigated for possible wrongdoing. The investigation only took four months. In July 1998 the Inspector General gave her report indicating significant evidence of criminal wrongdoing. The Justice Department ignored the report until March of 2000, giving the appearance the Inspector General was still investigating. In reality the department was just stalling. On March 28, 2000 the Justice Department told the Pentagon it would not prosecute anyone ("Update on Linda Tripp File Case").

The Justice Department gave three ridiculous excuses for its conclusion. It defended Assistant Secretary of Defense for Public Affairs Bacon, arguing he only released part of Tripp's confidential file not all of it. Deputy Inspector General Donald Mancuso said that criminal abuses of the Privacy Act do not depend on the amount released ("Update on Linda Tripp File Case"). This DOJ argument was outrageous. It implicitly gives the federal government permission to release any citizen's social security number. After all that is only part of a confidential file.

Justice also claimed the Freedom of Information Act takes priority over the Privacy Act. Well, for starters that's not true. One's privacy prevails over the media's right to know, as the Freedom of Information Act's exemptions relating to personal privacy indicate. Even if the Department of Justice's argument was valid, the explanation failed because no one filed a timely request under the Freedom of Information Act ("Update on Linda Tripp File Case").

The Justice Department also stated that it would not prosecute because Bacon "'didn't intend to break the law'" ("Update on Linda Tripp File Case"). Common sense would also reject this argument. If a person gets stopped for speeding and says that he did not mean to go over the speed limit, the police officer isn't going to smile and let that person go ("Update on Linda Tripp File Case"). Criminal intent can be inferred by the action itself.

According to the Inspector General, Bacon broke the law. The Justice Department declined prosecution giving three weak excuses that common sense refuted. It seems the Justice Department protected Bacon refusing to hold him accountable for the release of Tripp's information. Most likely the release entailed more than just a violation of the Privacy Act. At the time, Linda Tripp was a major threat and enemy of the Clinton White House. Was the leak designed to discredit her and was it tantamount to obstruction of justice?

Chances are Bacon did not act on his own because people in public affairs are warned not to release confidential information (Nordlinger, "Why Didn't Bacon Get Fried"). A trial might have told the true circumstances surrounding the release. Why did Bacon do it? Who orchestrated it? A trial might have provided answers, but once again it appears Justice was looking for anything but answers. The release of the documents helped only Bill Clinton because Tripp was a threat to him and this would impeach her credibility. No one else had anything to gain. As usual Clinton would stay above the fray; another fortuitous event had spared him accountability.

Willey Letters and Justice

The Justice Department did all it could to help Clinton when he violated Kathleen Willey's privacy as a way to discredit her. The Honorable Judge Lamberth ruled that Clinton and his top lawyers were in violation of the law. The ruling allowed Judicial Watch to access additional information regarding White House involvement in the release of the Willey letters, which it could use for the FileGate lawsuit (Garrett, "Appeals Court to hear arguments in Willey case").

A judge ruled that the President of the United States broke the law. The Justice Department should have attempted to punish the violators of the Privacy Act whose efforts to discredit Willey may have obstructed justice. The Justice Department should have appointed a separate independent counsel. Justice did get involved but on the wrong side of the matter. It did everything it could to be a thorn in the side of Judicial Watch.

Government lawyers asked the appeals court to overturn Lamberth's decision that Clinton violated the Privacy Act. They argued that the Privacy Act does not effect the president. (Garrett, "Appeals Court to hear arguments in Willey case").

Reno's Justice Department acted inappropriately. What we continually see in many of these cases is the president using federal employees, from aides to department heads, and the unlimited resources provided by taxpayer funds to defend and protect the president. This was sometimes appropriate but other times not. Taxpayer funds are not the private piggy bank of the executive. In this case the Justice Department's legal argument was not upheld but the delaying tactics were most helpful to the administration. Of course, no one was ever held responsible for leaking the information.

The efforts of the Justice Department were a nice try to protect Clinton. For Janet Reno it was business as usual, except for anyone who lacked ties to the Clinton Administration. We were living in a Clintonocracy. For eight years the Clintons trampled on and manipulated all the executive levers of government. Even the famous, wealthy, powerful, and well-connected are not above the law, unless their name was Clinton. While others were affected by the laws, the Clintons were the law.

Knowlton and Justice

Patrick Knowlton unfortunately went to Fort Marcy Park on the day Vince Foster died. He claimed he was subsequently stalked and had his car destroyed under unusual circumstance the night before his second FBI interview. A limousine driver happened to witness the destruction of Knowlton's car and got the aggressor's license plate. A private investigator discovered the assailant was Scott Jeffrey Bickett, an employee at the Department of Defense with a top U.S. security clearance. Bickett confessed, but the Office of the United States Attorney for the District of Columbia refused requests to prosecute. ("Ft. Marcy Park Witness Patrick Knowlton Lawsuit").

Bickett intentionally violated Knowlton's property rights and was caught. This was not an accident. The bashing of Knowlton's car appeared illegal and is certainly not acceptable behavior for those with active top secret clearance. I think that Bickett's actions went beyond ordinary vandalism. The day after this occurrence, Knowlton had his second FBI interview. There is at least a possibility that Bickett's actions attempted to intimidate Knowlton and obstruct justice. One can speculate that Bickett did not act out of the blue on his own volition. Why would a Defense Department employee do such a thing, possibly endangering his position? Did someone put him up to it? Maybe it was just another coincidence.

What it all means and where it leads, I do not know. Certainly the Justice Department demonstrated little interest in pursuing the matter and doing its job. The case was soon closed. Best to leave sleeping dogs lie, I guess! Justice at the least should have investigated Bickett to ascertain his motivation and if any of this did, in fact, relate to Foster's death. Could it be the Department might have known where the investigation led and decided to terminate the inquiry?

Campaign Finance Investigation and Justice

Another egregious example of Janet Reno's partisanship was her response to the campaign fundraising activities of Al Gore and Bill Clinton. The Independent Counsel Law required an attorney general to appoint an independent counsel if the president, vice president, or certain top White House officials perpetrated apparent malfeasance. The law existed because the attorney general, as a political appointee, has an inherent conflict of interest making it impossible for him or her to investigate objectively. With respect to the 1996 Clinton-Gore campaign evidence indicated wrongdoing, but Reno doggedly refused to appoint an independent counsel despite the recommendation of her top lieutenants (Olson, "The Most Political Justice Department Ever: A Survey").

Reno argued she based her decision on the opinions of career prosecutors. However that was not true. FBI Director Louis Freeh and other top FBI officials wrote to Reno in support of the appointment of an independent counsel. Charles La Bella, head of the fundraising investigation, Robert Lit of the Criminal Divisions, a staunch Democrat and a Clinton friend, and Robert Conrad, the head of the fundraising task force, all recommended the appointment of an independent counsel (Olson, "The Most Political Justice Department Ever: A Survey").

Reno initially claimed she did not appoint an independent

counsel because Gore 's phone calls on government property raised soft money, which according to Reno was legal. Once it was established the calls on government property did raise hard money, Reno argued Gore unknowingly violated the law. Consequently, an independent counsel was not necessary. Leon Panetta, however, testified that Gore listened to discussions pertaining to the hard money fundraising. Although evidence now existed Gore broke the law and did it knowingly, Reno still refused, saying "'there is no evidence that he heard the statements [about the hard money] or understood their implications'" (Olson, "The Most Political Justice Department Ever: A Survey").

Reno's actions were strange. Usually an attorney general does not have time to get involved personally in a case and accepts the recommendations of her top aides, but in this investigation Reno made the decision herself, ignoring the advice of everyone. She overlooked possible campaign finance abuses and the Independent Counsel Law. I think Reno wanted to conduct the investigation herself to prevent a fair and unbiased investigation. She wanted to insure those at the top got off.

Reno not only ignored her top advisers, she constantly stonewalled and delayed. She refused to cooperate with congressional subpoenas. Burton's Committee on Government Reform and Oversight subpoenaed the Freeh and La Bella notes, but Reno did not turn them over. Both reports indicated laws may have been broken and the necessity for an Independent Counsel investigation. Burton needed the documents in his capacity as Chairman to investigate possible wrongdoing, which is the committee's mandate. Reno would not comply because they contained grand jury testimony. Yet, the subpoena did not request any grand jury information and Freeh stated they contained little such testimony (Burton, "Burton Rejects Reno's Reasons for Withholding LaBella and Freeh Memos").

This was an example of common sense and the facts coinciding. She was protecting those at the top. Four (current or retired) FBI agents testified how the Justice Department blocked their attempts to scrutinize the Clinton-Gore campaign finance scandal. FBI agents testified that for four months top Justice Department officials, Laura Ingersoll, head of the Justice Department's campaign finance task force, and Lee Radek, head of Public Integrity, impeded requests to obtain a warrant to search Charlie Trie's office. While the Justice Department blocked the agents, Trie shredded valuable documents. Agents who looked through Trie's trash discovered records subpoenaed by Senator Thompson's Committee ("Obstruction of Justice Department").

The torn up Trie documents included photographs of six checks from Asian contributors to President Clinton's legal defense fund. Agents also discovered Democratic National Committee donor lists and a Federal Express document indicating Trie mailed two pounds of documents to the White House in May of 1997. Other documents showed the White House had informed Trie about the investigation into his activities. The checks to the Clinton's defense fund were suspicious, but the Justice Department told the FBI that "'we will not pursue this matter'" ("Obstruction of Justice Department").

Even stranger were the Justice Department's decisions about the FBI pulling over a car. In July 1997 agents witnessed a man remove documents from Trie's house and bring them to the home of Maria Mapili, Trie's business manager. The FBI convinced Public Integrity at Justice to pull over the car, but once it learned the man was Mr. Mapili's lawyer, Justice revoked the FBI's right to stop the car ("Obstruction of Justice Department").

Remember when President Bush nominated Ashcroft as Reno's successor, the Democrats and the major media instantly questioned whether this devote man would enforce the laws fairly for all. Well, where were they for eight years when we heard not a peep, let alone preemptive concern?

ChinaGate and Justice

Illegal money is one thing. Bribery is another. Serious allegations demand serious investigations, but Justice Department officials once again seemed reluctant to investigate. The Justice Department had the perfect stepping stones to uncover the truth. They had the goods on Huang, Chung, Riady, and Trie. If a Clinton China connection existed, they knew about it. The Justice Department held the sword of Damocles. Yet, rather than using the leverage, it let them go. The Justice Department should have put pressure on them in exchange for a reduced sentence or immunity. They might have explained their motives for donating illegal money and anything received in return. The late Honorable Judge Sirica did this in WaterGate, threatening to throw the book at the wrongdoers. The media loved it at the time. Something tells me they wouldn't have loved it circa 1993 through 2000.

The DOJ ignored this tried and true prosecutorial practice giving Trie, Huang, Riady, and Chung no reason to cooperate. They did not spend a single day in jail. The Justice Department did not put any pressure on them to talk, so except for Chung, they did not. If unwinding the imbroglio was a priority, the Department of Justice had a solid model to follow. Instead it did just the opposite.

John Huang, a key figure in ChinaGate, allegedly transferred U.S. secrets. The Department of Justice only sentenced him to a fine and community service. He was not punished for the $1.6 million he illegally raised. The Justice Department decided to only punish him for two illegal contributions to two California campaigns in 1993 and 1994. Huang seemed a great lead to pursue, but Justice Department gave him a slap on the wrist and promised not to punish him further, effectively removing all pressure for him to talk (Kondracke, "GOP must launch new probe of Chinagate").

Huang could have talked about phone calls he made after seeing top secret documents, Lippo's connections to Chinese Intelligence, money paid to Tucker and Hubbell, and how he acquired his position at Commerce. Certainly one could expect a vigorous prosecution to seek answers to these issues. It was not to be. The DOJ made life easy for Huang, but predominantly it kept the bright lights off the Clintons.

Charlie Trie received a similar sweet deal from the Justice

Department. Although he was not cooperating with Congress nor the DOJ, the Department of Justice recommended he get only three years probation. It recommended no fine, no community service, and no jail time. Usually sentences in plea bargains are based on the cooperation of the person, but the Justice Department did not want to wait to see if Trie cooperated. He pled guilty in June, but the Justice Department expedited the sentencing date for early August. Over staunch Justice Department opposition, Congressman Dan Burton had the sentencing date postponed until after Trie cooperated with Congress (Burton, "Opening Statement Chairman Dan Burton Committee on Government Reform").

Why did the Justice Department want to sentence Trie before he cooperated? Possibly so Trie would have no motive to talk. The Justice Department's actions demonstrated their reluctance for Trie to cooperate. The Department of Justice should have wanted Trie to talk in order to learn about possible corruption. If all this sound fishy, stay tuned.

In March of 2000, the Justice Department further undermined Trie's value by refusing to grant Trie immunity. It only granted him limited immunity, meaning he would have to testify at his own risk. When the head of the Campaign Finance Task Force, Robert Conrad refused to grant full immunity, he prevented Trie from telling all for fear of self-incrimination ("Conrad Also Tries to Throw 'Monkey Wrench' Into Lamberth's ChinaGate Court Proceeding").

If the Justice Department seriously wanted to investigate, it would not have fought Trie's testimony and granted him immunity. With immunity Trie might have clarified many unanswered questions. The Justice Department did everything in its jurisdiction to keep Trie quiet, essentially closing the lid on another Clinton scandal. One has to wonder why not grant full immunity. Based on other related deals cut by the government, there was no indication serious punishment was in store for Trie anyway.

James Riady also got a friendly plea agreement that took away his value to prosecutors. The billionaire was ordered to pay $8.6 million but got no jail time. Riady received a light punishment not consistent with his serious illegal actions (Whitcomb, "Clinton Friend Riady Pleads Guilty, Fined $8.6 million). Riady was possibly the most valuable witness. He could have told the authorities about the money he gave to Tucker and Hubbell and the possible quid pro quo for his generous donations to Bill Clinton. The Justice Department could have used Riady to unearth the truth behind numerous Clinton scandals but instead insured his silence by subverting justice.

Let me be technically correct. It is true this Riady plea was sealed under the incoming Bush administration which accepted the agreement entered into by its predecessor. It appears that the new administration rightly or wrongly has decided not to revisit any old cans of worms left over from the Clinton years. I suppose Bush does not want to be diverted from his own agenda by being sidetracked into some no win liberal media blitz about "playing politics" etc., etc.

Emails and Justice

In March of 2000 the Justice Department launched a criminal investigation into the missing White House emails. The investigation was needed because the emails contained sensitive, possibly incriminating, information about the Clintons' activities. The issue was whether the failure to store over one hundred thousand emails comprised an honest mistake or obstruction of justice.

Some rightfully reproached the investigation. Indiana Congressman Dan Burton was skeptical and wrote Reno, "'You cannot use the Campaign Financing Task Force, supervised by yourself, to investigate yourself and the Justice Department lawyers who helped to keep the emails from being produced'" (NewsMax staff, "Burton Tells Reno to Clear Her Skirts"). Burton wanted an independent counsel appointed. Reno never appointed one (NewsMax staff, "Burton Tells Reno to Clear Her Skirts").

Others criticized the timing of Reno's decisions, believing she was attempting to prevent Judicial Watch from obtaining information detrimental to the Clintons and stall until after the election (NewsMax staff, "Burton Tells Reno to Clear Her Skirts").

The concerns about Reno's objectivity were well grounded. Initially the Justice Department promised to complete the investigation in sixty to ninety days. Almost two months into the investigation, Robert Conrad had not even contacted the two main whistle-blowers in the email case ("More Justice Department Antics"). This seems to indicate the true nature of this sham investigation. The Justice Department was in no hurry.

A serious investigation might have yielded definitive findings, but none resulted from this "investigation." Reno clearly lacked objectivity. A couple of White House email contractors testified about alleged threats that White House personnel leveled. The White House aides swore their innocence. One group obviously lied under oath. Reno should have pursued this case.

The familiar puzzle was again presented. Who was telling the truth? Who was lying? Who had something to gain and someone to protect? Who had no vested interest? The usual smoke screen was employed diverting attention from what was being searched for to who was doing the searching. It was all too predictable. Remember this is not an eighteen minute gap in the Watergate tapes. This is hundreds of thousands of internal executive emails over a period of months missing in violation of statutory law. There are credible allegations of heavy-handed interference with all attempts to retrieve them. Needless to say it all proved too much for the Reno Justice Department—or maybe she was indeed fulfilling her job description. The issue never received much public attention and faded off into oblivion, easily dying a quiet death.

EmailGate was a serious scandal with no one held accountable. Any young person seriously following these events can only shake his or her head in disbelief. Can it really be this easy to game the system? Throw a load of pollution up against the establishment and enough sticks so one can pretty much get away with anything. What in the world are parents trying to teach? Times have changed and they are out of their depth. Don't bet on it! Remember there is the Clinton way and the right way.

Nolanda Hill and Justice

It is reassuring to know the Justice Department did not sleep through the entire eight years of Clinton's presidency. When Clinton was not the issue, for the most part it did its job. There were times during the Clinton presidency, however, the Justice Department exhibited over zealousness in its haste to discredit and bully Clinton enemies.

On January 28, 1998, Nolanda Hill reluctantly filed a sealed affidavit indicating her knowledge about high level Clinton officials' selling the trade missions and suggesting evidence of obstruction of justice. She feared vengeance but still came forward ("Reno Justice Department Retaliates Against Witness in Clinton Fundraising Scandal").

On March 13, 1998 her fears became a reality when the Clinton Justice Department indicted her. Larry Klayman, Judicial Watch's Chairman, accused Bruce Heygi, a lawyer at the U.S Attorney's Office, of leaking Hill's affidavit to the Justice Department. This was not denied. Klayman also uncovered evidence that showed the Justice Department knew about the affidavit before the indictment ("Reno Justice Department Retaliates Against Witness in Clinton Fundraising Scandal").

The indictment came ten days before Hill was to testify about alleged administration improprieties. The indictment attempted to impede her testimony, forcing her to take the Fifth Amendment to prevent self-incrimination regarding information she learned through her relationship with the late Commerce Secretary Ron Brown ("Judicial Watch, Inc. vs. United States Department of Commerce").

The Justice Department bypassed the normal process with the Hill indictment, thus giving the appearance it was trying to deter her testimony. The Justice Department usually informs people they are targets of investigation before bringing indictments but not in this case. At her arraignment the Clinton Justice Department admitted it lacked the time to create an inventory of evidence against her. The rushed indictment appeared orchestrated to prevent testimony

("Judicial Watch, Inc. vs. United States Department of Commerce").

Bill Clinton had a good reason to prevent Hill's testimony. Hill courageously testified trade missions were sold, and she saw documents so indicating. Hill also testified that Hillary Clinton plotted the scheme and President Clinton, Vice President Gore, and many other White House officials covered it up ("Reno Justice Department Retaliates Against Witness in Clinton Fundraising Scandal"). Hill took a great risk in testifying. For this the Clinton Justice Department rewarded her with a re-indictment and re-arraignment claiming a typographical error in the original filings. Most likely the real reason was retaliation ("Judicial Watch, Inc. vs. United States Department of Commerce").

The Justice Department should have welcomed Hill's testimony and looked into her allegations. Finally someone was talking, but Janet Reno was not listening. It seems she used her power to stymie Hill's evidence by re-indicting her. Janet Reno did not want the truth about the Clintons, so her department discredited the rare cooperating witness. Reno insured that the Clintons were not held accountable. In view of the light sentences previously meted out to all Clinton related players the government had the goods on, why for heavens sake would the Department of Justice be silencing this one?

Tripp and Justice

Although the Justice Department was reluctant to proceed in matters related to the violation of Linda Tripp's privacy, State authorities had no problem indicting her on two charges dealing with her recording phone conversations with Monica Lewinsky. One charge dealt with the actual recording and the second charge dealt with her releasing the conversations to Newsweek (Associated Press, "Tripp indicted for wiretapping in Maryland").

Tripp's indictment resembled political payback for disclosing the affair which ultimately resulted in the impeachment of President Clinton. Tripp's attorneys argued authorities lacked a basis for the indictment because the independent counsel had granted Linda

Tripp immunity in 1998. The investigation, indictment, and prosecution stemmed from evidence acquired through the immunity agreement. The State prosecutors eventually dismissed the indictment in May of 2000 (Murtha, "Statement of Joseph Murtha Lead Criminal Defense Attorney For Linda R. Tripp").

Prosecutors could not have convicted Tripp. They had the impossible task of proving no evidence came from Tripp's Lewinsky testimony under a grant of immunity and that this testimony did not influence witnesses (Levin, "The Failed Political Prosecution"). Usually if prosecutors do not believe they can not get a conviction, they do not indict. Tripp was made an exception; they pursued her relentlessly.

Not only was the indictment groundless, but according to her lawyers, the State's investigation of Tripp differed from all others involving the violation of Maryland's wiretap law. The special assigned prosecutor received access to all State resources. This was an unusual measure for a wire tap investigation, especially since prosecutions for wiretap allegations are rare in Maryland (Murtha, "Statement of Joseph Murtha Lead Criminal Defense Attorney For Linda R. Tripp").

Tripp uncovered malfeasance and the Clinton support team attacked her mercilessly. One would think that the legal system would have kept its objectivity, but it did not. Maryland Democrats made Tripp pay for bringing the Monica Lewinsky scandal to light. One could easily speculate on the motives behind the indictment. I find it hard to believe that Maryland released the pit bulls on Tripp without at least tacit approval from the Feds.

The authorities should have worked with Tripp to ascertain the facts. Instead, the State of Maryland assumed the lead in discrediting her. Thereby making her the issue rather than Clinton. It has been said that a prosecutor can obtain an indictment of a hamburger, if he or she is intent on doing so! I guess this is especially true when that hamburger is deemed a threat to the Clintons.

Starr and Justice

The Clinton Justice Department also hindered Independent Counsel Ken Starr's investigation. On the one hand Reno granted expansions to the investigation at Starr's request, while simultaneously undermining him by filing briefs in opposition to Starr's investigation. For example, she filed a brief supporting the White House's claim government lawyers who met with Hillary Clinton should not have to turn over their notes. The Justice Department also backed the administration's position that Secret Service agents did not have to testify regarding information they witnessed. Although a judge threw both claims out, the net effect was delay and loss of prosecutorial momentum (Olson, "The Most Political Justice Department Ever: A Survey"). One can wonder whether that was not the intent in the first place.

The Justice Department did not need to involve itself in this manner. By filing the amicus curiae briefs she effectively thwarted Starr's investigation. This provides further evidence as to what her true mission was in many of these investigations.

As Clinton's impeachment commenced in the Senate, Reno launched an investigation into Starr. No new allegations or evidence prompted the investigation. The timing raised the possibility the ploy was little more than a veiled attempt to discredit him on the eve of Clinton's impeachment (Suro, "U.S. Advised Starr of Probe Last Month").

The investigation of Starr slowly dragged on and dampened Starr's effectiveness as a prosecutor. There should have been an expedited investigation. If Starr had abused his power, Janet Reno should have fired him. If he broke the law, he should have lost his position. Water torture was the strategy. Reno did nothing. She let the investigation plod on. This strategy helped Bill Clinton (Frieden, "Hatch Demands Conclusion to Justice Probe of Starr"). In the end Starr, who is an honorable man, was cleared. The Justice Department's lengthy investigation, however, tainted his credibility and impaired his effectiveness, especially in the court of public opinion.

Reno was a continual thorn in Starr's side. Her actions helped to delay the impeachment and secure survival for Clinton. Usually the authorities work together to convict the wrongdoers, with the Clintons it was the other way around.

It is ironic how all this played out. Starr emerges with his reputation somewhat bruised and battered. Reno survives with possible future political ambitions intact. Even U.S. attorneys, like Mary Jo White, are probably in line for handsome positions in the next Democratic administration.

Summary

Janet Reno played an essential part in helping the Clintons evade responsibility for their actions. In a partisan manner she abused her power to abet the Clintons. She was willing to release her pit bulls to discredit a whistle-blower when necessary but went easy on Clinton confidants within her departmental sites.

We have speculated on the Clintons' modus operandi, using under-the-table deals and intimidation. Is that how the Clintons kept Reno in check? In Clinton's first term, Reno appointed a number of independent counsels to examine suspicious practices. In the second term, however, she was reluctant to appoint them and refused to appoint one to investigate the administration's most serious questionable actions, the campaign finance abuses. Was this a coincidence or did it have to do with the fact Reno was the last Cabinet member Clinton re-appointed for a second term? The Clintons were angry over the number of independent counsels appointed, and Reno desperately wanted to stay on for a second term. In the end both parties got what they wanted.

Reno's actions contributed to the survival of the Clinton presidency. Furthermore, she helped to create a false self-confidence for us young people. Kids love to push the envelope to see how much they can get away with. They think they are invincible. She demonstrated to all how one can survive and prosper with a little help from a friend. It was the most cynical example for my generation that it's who you know, not whether you do right or wrong that is the ultimate barometer of success. In the end I believe she forgot that the attorney general is the peoples' attorney, not the private handmaiden of the president.

Reno's Justice Department was Bill Clinton's personal legal defense fund that all U.S. taxpayers (rich, poor, liberal, conservative) were compelled to support. Reno allowed Clinton to teach us young people that anything is possible. Any actions can be done with virtually no repercussions. Unfortunately, the lesson is misleading. The Clintons' lifestyle was viable for them but would not work for others. In the end most people get caught and pay a significant penalty. Young people must understand that even the Clintons could not have gotten off the hook without help, such as that provided by Janet Reno.

Clinton was not the first president who tried to manipulate the Justice Department. President Nixon comes to mind. For whatever reason, however, the media appeared more vigilant in the 1970's than during the Clinton terms. I am going to guess politics had something to do with it.

Chapter 12
The Not So Objective Media

If the media had done its job, Janet Reno could have delayed, stonewalled, and rejected all the obviously needed independent counsels she wanted, and the Clintons still might not have survived. One of the media's jobs is to inform the public about corruption. When the media sees something that is not right, they should objectively inform the public. In the proper forum they should editorialize, investigate, and lead the search for truth and accountability. When wrongdoing exists, the media should raise public awareness and expose the issues in an effort to eliminate it. The media did this effectively in the WaterGate scandal. They rightfully rallied public support for the truth, ultimately leading to the resignation of Richard Nixon.

The media aggressively informed the public about the Nixon scandal. By contrast, during the Clinton years, filled with numerous serious scandals, the media largely looked the other way. The media did not properly inform the public. They did not investigate or demand answers with the same vigor. Obviously some forms of the media gave adequate coverage and tried to ascertain the facts. Most did not, including the most influential network news programs. Yes, one could check the <u>Wall Street Journal</u> or occasionally find an article in the <u>New York Times</u>, but that is almost irrelevant because most people do not read them. The average person does not have the time to scrutinize the editorial pages of the paper to see what law the president might have broken today. He or she usually just sits down in front of the television after a hard day of work and at most watches a network evening news program to learn the day's events.

The media has tremendous influence and during the Clinton presidency that power helped save the Clintons. The media did not do their job adequately. If they had, an informed electorate would have created a public uproar against the Clintons' actions. Nonsense excuses involving the vice president's excessive drinking of iced tea, numerous unexplained bureaucratic errors, or lying to one's diary would not have been permitted to slide by, if covered at all. Public opinion would have allowed independent counsels to have been more effective and less timid. For example, it appeared ample evidence existed for indictments in the FileGate scandal and more in the Whitewater scandal. Since the media did not highlight some of the underhanded tactics earlier described, however, the demand for accountability and public support did not suffice. Accordingly, Starr only indicted those he was extremely confident a jury could convict. Thus, there were fewer indictments and even fewer answers.

The majority of people working for the media are liberals. For example, eighty-nine percent of Washington reporters voted for Bill Clinton in 1992 ("The Stats"). The media's liberal beliefs are acceptable because everyone has opinions, but the media's liberal bias is not. In my opinion, the media put its politics ahead of its responsibility to report objectively. Certainly the vigor of investigative reporting of the WaterGate affair was missing. This lax reporting helped the Clintons escape a never ending stream of connected allegations and scandals. Much of what the Clintons did was not simply inappropriate or fishy, but they survived and were able to do pretty much whatever they wanted. This teaches impressionable kids that they can ignore their parents' advice, especially on issues of character, honor, altruism, and respect, just like the Clintons did. There is just one problem, they can't. If those kids get in trouble or are under suspicion, the media and the authorities will do their jobs to see that the truth is known and those who wronged are punished. The Clintons' lessons to children are specious because John Q. Public does not have the benefit of such an accommodative media.

Broaddrick and the Media

Juanita Broaddrick conveyed some shocking allegations against President Clinton. Although she had more credibility than Clinton by the time she went public, and despite others confirming much of her claim, the media did not create a clamor over the fact that the President of the United States was accused of rape.

Reporters for the New York Times and the Los Angeles Times first heard allegations about Broaddrick near the end of the 1992 presidential campaign. However, both newspapers decided not to write a story (Barringer, "On Tortuous Route, Sexual Assault Accusation Against Clinton Resurfaces").

The public had a right to know whether a presidential hopeful had done something as cruel and criminal as raping someone. This is the type of story all news outlets should have investigated and reported to the public. It's not the media's job to establish guilt or innocence, but once the story proved credible, the media should have run with it. One would think that kind of investigative, factual journalism might have won someone a Pulitzer, but instead reporters backed off. Informing the public would have hurt Clinton and cost him votes, so the public was left in the dark.

The allegation lingered until Broaddrick came forward in 1999. Broaddrick agreed to do an interview with Lisa Myers who had requested the interview for over a year. The interview occurred on January 20, 1999 (two weeks into the Senate impeachment trial) and was scheduled to air on the January 29, 1999 episode of "Dateline." Although, NBC investigated the story thoroughly, NBC did not air it, saying it was still a "work in progress." NBC had four witnesses. What else did they need? (Rabinowitz, "Wall Street Journal Editorial Commentary-Juanita Broaddrick Meets the Press). Was it responsible journalism, or protecting their own?

NBC had a huge story but was reluctant to air it. It appeared the higher ups did not want the public to hear this one for fear of prejudicing Clinton at the impeachment trial. NBC had no reason to sit on the story. Yes, journalists must check their sources and be careful not to spread lies, but a station normally would air a timely newsworthy story that checks out. In fact there would be pressure for a station to air their story first. At least that is how it usually works. Journalists air a story and then do follow ups. The media should have given the Broaddrick story maximum exposure, thus enhancing the likelihood someone else might come forward with more information. However, NBC did not want to hurt the Clinton presidency, so the station refrained. The networks sure did not need much investigative time before blasting away with the thoroughly unsubstantiated Anita Hill allegation.

The story eventually broke through the media's wall. The credible allegation was a major story that investigative journalists should have pounced upon to bring Broaddrick justice. However, once the allegation came forward, the media still largely ignored it.

According to the Media Research Center the first five days after the Broaddrick story broke, the evening news of ABC, CBS, CNN, NBC, and PBS devoted just two stories to the devastating allegation. The morning coverage was no better. Only NBC's "Today" and "Good Morning America" briefly mentioned the allegation. Broaddrick's allegation was more serious than Anita Hill's allegation about Clarence Thomas' alleged and uncorroborated inappropriate language. However, in the five days after the breaking of Hill's allegation, those same five main evening news stations did a total of sixty-seven stories on Hill's allegation, and the morning shows for the first five days gave it sixty-six stories and eighteen interviews. In the first five days after the breaking news, Hill got 151 stories compared to the mere four about Broaddrick ("Why the

Difference?").

Bill O'Reilly asked CBS news anchor Dan Rather about the lack of coverage the issue got. Rather claimed not to be too familiar with the case, but when O'Reilly reminded Rather, Rather said that it was part of a Republican campaign to get Clinton. According to Rather the allegation was a "'private sex life'" issue not warranting coverage ("Juanita Broaddrick: Dan Rather's Comments 'Sickened Me'").

Rape is a terrible thing, but as Broaddrick says, "'it becomes more difficult when someone such as Dan Rather makes such frivolous statements about the most horrific event of my life'" ("Juanita Broaddrick: Dan Rather's Comments 'Sickened Me'").

Everyone has political beliefs, including journalists, and that is fine. The problem is that unless they are doing clearly identified editorials, they have an obligation to report fairly and objectively. They should subrogate their personal beliefs. From Rather's comments it is obvious his beliefs affect his reporting. Anyone who thinks that rape is a "private" issue is spinning. Perhaps, Mr. Rather should give up his "day job" and continue giving keynote speeches at Democratic fund-raisers or officially become a Democratic spinner.

The media failed to do its job in the Broaddrick matter. They did not adequately inform or search for the truth. In fact, the media basically ignored the scandal. To this day, the public is not aware of the established facts behind the allegation. Most people probably never even heard the allegations, especially if Dan Rather's claim not to be too familiar with the case is true. Witnesses and credibility support Broaddrick, but the media refrained from digging too deep. What were they afraid of, besides the truth? Certainly, the media did not give the benefit of the doubt to Clarence Thomas and would not give it to you. Do I hear political agenda?

Kathleen Willey and the Media

Unlike with Broaddrick, the national media did discuss Kathleen Willey, albeit, not with fair, objective coverage. Evidence supporting her claim of groping and intimidation received far less attention than contradictory evidence.

On Monday night, March 16, 1998 all of the networks began their news shows with significant coverage of the White House spin on the Willey letters. The media made a big deal about the friendliness in Willey's letters to Clinton as contradicting proof of her allegation. Only NBC's Lisa Myers presented a sexual harassment expert who stressed that just because she stayed friendly with President Clinton did not mean she lied about her claim (Baker, "Willey's Weak Credibility?; Flowers Found; Emma Thompson; Yes to Clinton").

All of the stations aired comments of Ann Lewis, a White House political operative, doubting Willey's allegation due to her friendliness. On ABC's "World News Tonight" Lewis said that Willey's allegation "'Simply is contradicted by the person I met with who in 1996 was so positive about the President'" (Baker, "Willey's Weak Credibility?; Flowers Found; Emma Thompson; Yes to Clinton").

All the networks used Lewis to discredit Willey, but only ABC reminded viewers how Lewis hypocritically used the exact opposite reasoning to support Anita Hill in 1991. In 1991 Lewis said, "'We know what it's like to work for a boss who insults you, who degrades you and yet you feel you have to go on working, you have to go on working, you have to go on being friendly'" (Baker, "Willey's Weak Credibility?; Flowers Found; Emma Thompson; Yes to Clinton").

Two sides exist to every issue. However, the networks used the letters solely to refute Willey's claim. These networks were concerned with spreading an agenda rather than spreading news, no pun intended.

When a judge ruled Clinton and his aides broke the law by releasing the letters, the story received only nominal coverage before being relegated to oblivion on some back pages. On Wednesday March 29, 2000 MSNBC devoted ten minutes talking about flammable mattresses, NBC spent five minutes discussing Tony Blair's wife requesting he take a paternity leave, and CNN devoted two minutes explaining a correlation between the length of a woman's index finger and whether or not she is a lesbian. Obviously, not that much happened on March 29, so ample time existed to explain the Willey case and the judge's ruling, still the network evening news programs gave the ruling very little coverage. The network evening news programs combined gave the ruling a mere sixty-six seconds while CNN's "The World Today" only spent twenty-eight seconds and MSNBC's "The News with Brian Williams" only twenty-three seconds (Baker, "Seconds for Clinton's "Criminal Violation"; Ruling Buried at Press Conference").

A judge ruling that the President of the United States broke a law does not happen everyday—even by Clinton standards, so the ruling should have gotten considerable coverage at least comparable to the flurry of attention the letters received when released. The net result diminished Willey's credibility from the ensuing publicity, but the all too familiar deafening silence following the court ruling spared Clinton. The media speculated and drew conclusions about Willey's integrity when the White House released the letters, but when a judge ruled the release illegal, the networks did not speculate about Clinton's motive.

Further evidence the networks' intended to help Clinton escape Willey's allegation was the media's coverage of statements made by Jared Stern, a private investigator. Jackie Judd reported in a January 29, 1999 "World News Tonight" exclusive that Nathan Landow's lawyer hired Stern to investigate Willey, but in a conspicuous way so she would know. As we learned from the Knowlton experience, this is a technique to intimidate and terrify the target. Stern denied being the jogger that threatened Willey, but he believed one existed ("NewsBites").

This event had major implications, raising the possibility a close Gore friend hired a private investigator to intimidate Willey before her testimony in the Paula Jones case. The media should have given this story at least comparable exposure to the Willey letters. Questions related to this episode should have been asked of Clinton, Gore, and Landow about this harassment. Why did they want Willey silenced? Let's be clear. Stern is now backing up Willey's story, claiming Landow hired him to "investigate" Willey but in an overt obvious manner designed to induce fear as opposed to finding out information. He was employed to intimidate Willey, plain and simple!

The story was potentially explosive. All the media had to do was light the match and watch to see who blew up. Needless to say, the media was not interested. CBS, NBC, CNN, Newsweek, and U.S. News & World Report did not inform the public about the story. Only the Fox News Channel and Time, briefly in an article, mentioned the story ("NewsBites").

The wrongdoing and cover up in the Willey matter seemed apparent, but the media did not fairly report it, leaving the public uninformed. The media did not lead in the search for truth and accountability. By selective reporting they helped lay the allegations to rest.

Paula Jones and the Media

In my favorite sport, baseball, if you are batting and the pitcher throws the ball outside, a pitch the umpire has called a ball the entire game, but this time the umpire calls a strike; you assume the umpire made an honest mistake. You step back in the batter's box and the pitcher pitches again. This time the ball is a little further outside and the umpire again calls the pitch a strike. You start to get suspicious of the umpire. However, you are still open-minded and think that possibly it was a coincidence or maybe the umpire just wasn't paying attention. You step back up to the plate hoping for a fair call, hoping the strike zone will return to its precedent. The pitcher winds up and throws the ball even farther off the plate. You turn around confidently thinking you will see ball one signaled, but instead hear, "strike three." Clearly something has changed. Could it be the umpire is a friend of the new relief pitcher? Does the umpire want the game to end so he can go home and eat dinner with his wife? Does the umpire not like you or does he have a different reason? Regardless, obviously the calls were not accidents.

Well, objectivity just struck out looking. Paula Jones is the media's third strike. If the media's pro-liberal Clinton bias was not clear before, it is now. Anita Hill got endless favorable coverage supporting her unsubstantiated claims. The media refused to do this for Broaddrick, Willey, or Jones. Just like the strike zone, clearly the standards changed, but unlike the baseball analogy, the reason for the change was obvious.

Previously mentioned were the sixty-seven stories the evening news shows of ABC, PBS, CNN, NBS, and ABC gave Anita Hill's allegation in the first five days after going public. The networks led with her each day except CNN. CNN only used her as the lead story three times. Paula Jones' allegations only received one sixteen second story in the first five days after her allegation broke ("From I am Woman to Who's that Girl?").

Both Paula Jones and Anita Hill levied unsubstantiated claims of sexual harassment against powerful people. Jones' claim of Bill Clinton exposing himself and asking for oral sex blew away Hill's claim of Thomas' suggestive talk. If anything the media should have granted Paula Jones more coverage than Hill, but actually the coverage reversed logic. The media's coverage was not comparable and not fair. The media played up allegations against a conservative while it ignored allegations against a liberal. The media should have given both allegations at least comparable coverage to spur investigations into the allegations, but the media only did this for Hill. The media decided for its audience that Jones' allegations were not newsworthy. Not to appear too cynical but could it have anything to do with that identifying big "D" next to Clinton's name—you know, the membership card that says "you are one of us." Maybe it is not an intentional bias. It could be collectively mainstream media folks are so left of center that they see contrary opinions curving off the charts to the right. The media has a responsibility to report objectively, and the public should get to draw its own conclusions. As for Paula Jones, the media was not taking any chances with this one!

The Constitution certainly provides and protects all our rights and privileges. Freedom of speech is one of the most basic and treasured by all Americans. It seems to me that because of the especially broad reach of the major media, they have a sacred responsibility to be objective, fair, balanced, and to carefully identify editorial comment. The media abdicated its responsibility as to Paula Jones' claim.

After ABC aired the initial Jones story on February 11, 1994, the networks did not mention her for two months. On May 4, 1994 The Washington Post finally printed a story on its investigation into the Jones affair prompting a story on CNN's "World News." Jones got some media coverage for the next couple of days, but nothing as extensive as the coverage given to Hill. Through May 9, 1994 Jones' allegations had only received sixteen evening stories and for the rest of the month only six more. From February 11, 1994 to the end of May, 1994 the evening news programs gave Paula Jones twenty-two stories, which was much less than the sixty-seven stories Hill received in the first five days ("From I am Woman to Who's that Girl?").

Not only did the amount of coverage bestowed on Hill and Jones differ, but the type of coverage differed too. When the networks reported on Jones, the coverage helped to discredit her. ABC's Jim Wooten ran a story using state pay records to contradict Jones' claim that the charges caused her to suffer professionally. The media never did investigative pieces attempting to prove Hill's allegation false ("From I am Woman to Who's that Girl?").

On May 8, 1994 ABC 's Sheilah Kast reported a poll indicating most Americans exhibited apathy towards Paula Jones ("From I am Woman to Who's that Girl?"). Most likely ABC ran the story in an attempt to further take any remaining wind out of its sails, insuring the story slipped away. It was no surprise that the majority of Americans did not care about Paula Jones because pretty much the media ignored her. Unlike Hill, the media did not elevate awareness of the allegations, so the story never took hold with the American public.

To further discredit Jones, the media questioned her reason for talking. ABC, NBC, and CNN all aired and helped publicize Clinton lawyer Robert Bennett's attacks on the personal and economic motives of Paula Jones. Comparable coverage was given to her sister's similar statements. None of the sixty-seven Anita Hill stories questioned her motives or even mentioned affidavits given to the Senate challenging Hill's motives and credibility ("From I am Woman to Who's that Girl?").

This schizophrenic spin in coverage between Hill and Jones also resonated in the morning news shows. The networks showed Hill as a victim whose vindication was imperative for our democracy and women's rights in particular, while the networks portrayed Jones as purely opportunistic, if not an outright liar. On the October 8, 1991 "Today" show, NBC reporter Andrea Mitchell said, "'What's at stake here and what is on trial, I think, is the Senate of the United States, that all-male institution but two'." This same show refused to grant Jones the same credibility. On the May 4, 1994 "Today" show Al Hunt of <u>The Wall Street Journal</u> said in reference to Jones, "'she has been used as sort of a puppet by the right, by the political right that wants to discredit Clinton, which I think certainly distracts from her credibility'" ("From I am Woman to Who's that Girl?").

The media normally reports the news to help discover the facts. Obviously the media had a double standard with President Clinton. They were willing to extend him every conceivable benefit of doubt. Accountability was on the back burner. If one of my classmates was alleged to have performed a similar stunt as Clinton did to Jones, the school newspaper would have instantly jumped all over the story as well as the local news and maybe with the national news wires in hot pursuit. No question, the girl would be portrayed as an innocent victim and instant, first impression, analysis would give a leg up on her story. I understand political correctness when I see it. Look I know, I am in school. Most guys are afraid to drop an innuendo, let alone their pants. The media would fall all over itself to obtain their perceived justice for the girl. Alleged Clinton-like behavior would be in the usual media terms consistent with today's liberal environment. The media would have no stake in the student's agenda and no reason to protect him. It's difficult to explain this disparity any other way.

Understand, I am not implicating a big media conspiracy. I highly doubt the Dan Rather, Tom Brokaw, Peter Jennings, and other media celebrities met clandestinely in some darkened Manhattan suite with the shades drawn and after checking the room for wiretaps, whispered agreement on how they could best save the Clinton presidency. In fact, the idea is farcical. Most likely the bias is subconscious. These media elites are predominately liberal, so in their minds Hill told the truth while Jones lied. Having these private opinions is acceptable but expressing them in hypnotic chant under the facade of "news" is not. That is what editorials are for.

Linda Tripp and the Media

The coverage mainstream media gave Linda Tripp resembled that extended to Kathleen Willey. The media did not thoroughly inform the public about Linda Tripp, thereby refusing to let people be informed or draw their own conclusions. That would have been much too objective and fair. The media did not care about Linda Tripp, but they did care about Bill Clinton. The same type of "coincidences" occurred. The public apparently had a right to know mostly that which would help Clinton. Information that discredited Tripp the media covered in depth, while information possibly detrimental to the Clintons did not receive nearly as much attention.

On July 7, 1998 all networks told the public a Maryland Grand Jury had been appointed to investigate if Tripp's tapings violated the law ("Who Said Linda Tripp had Rights?"). The media also gave substantial coverage to Linda Tripp's indictment. ABC's "World News Tonight," the "CBS Evening News," CNN's "The World," Fox News Channel's "Fox Report," and MSNBC's "The News with Brain Williams" each ran a full story on the indictment. "NBC Nightly news" also briefly mentioned the story (Baker, "CBS Bought Hillary's 'Candor'; $90,000 Skipped in AM; 'Stupid Tax Cut'").

The above stories were news and the media had every right to report them. My complaint is the media's double standard. If a grand jury investigates or indicts a person, that person is instantly discredited. However, if the person is exonerated, the media owe that person comparable time to restore one's name and credibility. The media decided against doing that for Linda Tripp.

Only the "Fox Report," of all the evening news shows, aired a full story on the decision to drop the Tripp case. "NBC Nightly News" ran a short blurb on it and MSNBC's "The News with Brain Williams" mentioned it briefly at the end of the show. CBS and ABC who both reported full stories about Tripp's indictment ignored her exoneration (Baker, "Tripp Trumped; Corroboration for Freeh Skipped; Erbe; Expect 'Conservatives to Lie'").

The news of Tripp's investigation and indictment got significantly more coverage than her vindication. Why was this? If the media wanted to tell the public everything significant about the Linda Tripp story, they would have given approximately equal coverage to the good and the bad, so the public could get a better idea of her true character. However, the media highlighted her trouble and ignored the positives. This raises the question: why did the media do this to Tripp and others who tried to hold the Clintons accountable? I believe the media played politics to garner support for their side, for the Clintons.

Normally a major news story culminates with blanket reporting and investigation. The media should have asked questions to get to the bottom of the Tripp indictment. Why was she indicted when granted federal immunity? Was the indictment political pay back? Widespread coverage of Tripp's exoneration could have helped her credibility vis-a-vis Clinton. Again the networks' decision as to what is newsworthy raises troubling questions of objectivity and motive.

This common sense conclusion is also supported by the media's coverage of the release of the contents in Tripp's private files. Every network reported the allegations that appeared in <u>The New Yorker</u> magazine, raising the possibility that Tripp lied on a federal application about an arrest ("Who Said Linda Tripp had Rights?").

However, all of the networks did not even report the Inspector General's ruling that the release of the files violated the Privacy Act. NBC and CBS evening news shows decided that their audiences did not have to know about it (Bozell, "Nothing New On the Clinton Women").

Information discrediting Tripp constituted major news, after all she provided hard evidence leading to impeachment. News that helped Tripp or showed possible government retaliation was barely newsworthy. NBC and CBS should have jumped on the story and investigated the release. Why did Bernath and Bacon really release the files? Why did the Justice Department and Defense Secretary Cohen basically ignore the ruling of the Inspector General? Why did they not take some meaningful action against Bernath and Bacon? Once again rather than trying to get to the bottom of this mystery, the media's attitude was let sleeping dogs lie. No Bernstein and Woodward on this caper.

The media had ample opportunity to ask questions. Defense Secretary Cohen was a guest on "Good Morning America," "This Week," "Face The Nation," "Today," "Meet the Press," and "NewsHour " from May 1998 to the beginning of October, but not one of these political shows bothered to bring up a single question about the Tripp file case ("Who Said Linda Tripp had Rights?"). The media clearly did not want to address this aspect of the scandal. Unlike the Nixon era, the media did not want answers so it avoided asking the right questions. Can you imagine Charles Colson in the WaterGate era appearing on these shows and not being grilled? The media did Clinton a great service, but set a poor example for the rest of us, especially children.

A person incriminates you and you retaliate by violating government procedures. The maliciousness seems obvious. The Clinton administration got away with it because of a complicitous, like-minded media. This like so many of the Clinton scandals was like a ladder, break the bottom and the rest would collapse under its own weight. The media put no pressure on those at the bottom, so the top never fell. This gives children the dual impression that it is easy to break laws, and character defamation is a good tactic to avoid responsibility. Both lessons are wrong. If the media had done its job with its usual vigor, the Clintons would not have emerged as celebrities. One does not have to be a brain surgeon to connect the dots, especially, when the same pattern is repeated over and again.

Look, it is true I am a kid, so maybe I am seeing things too black and white. Perhaps I am missing the subtleties and innuendoes in all of this. But that is exactly my point. We all know how important first impressions are. All these misdeeds and politically inspired accommodations left indelible marks on the psychic of many young people that will not easily, if ever be erased.

Ken Starr and the Media

Here's a good question for you. What is the difference between Ken Starr and the Tripp indictment? You might be fooled, but remember what chapter we are in. Yes, you guessed it. The difference was the media's coverage. During the Ken Starr's Clinton investigation, Democrats alleged a partisan vendetta. During the investigation of Linda Tripp, Republicans also alleged politically motivated scrutiny. In retrospect it seems Republicans had better grounds to complain. After all Starr's investigation lead to numerous indictments, convictions, and the unprecedented occurrence of a president coping a plea, essentially admitting perjury and accepting temporary disbarment to avoid prosecution upon leaving office.

When all was said and done, Starr's investigation had a legitimate and mandated purpose and obtained some degree of accountability while the investigation into Tripp went no where. Of course the media was not guided by the facts. Guess which investigation the media called partisan? It was not the Democratic prosecutor's trumped up indictment of a woman who received federal immunity to give evidence that led to the impeachment of a Democratic president. No, the partisanship was the investigation into whether the president committed illegal acts.

The media constantly ridiculed Starr and gave time and credence to Democratic anti-Starr spin. They always reminded the public that Starr was a Republican, but when the Tripp investigation began, the media did not inform the public that Maryland State Prosecutor Stephen Montanarelli was a Democrat ("Who Said Linda Tripp Had Rights"). Montanarelli did not receive the same grilling of partisan motives that Starr received although Montanarelli certainly had less of a case.

The network attacks on Starr included, but were certainly not limited to the following:

- On August 12, 1994 Dan Rather said, "'New disclosures are fueling questions about whether or not Starr is an ambitious Republican partisan backed by ideologically motivated anti-Clinton activists and judges from the Reagan, Bush, and Nixon years.'"
- On the September 17, 1996 "Today" show, Bryan Gumbel asked, "'Have you any doubt that Kenneth Starr and his deputies are pursuing an agenda that is purely political?'"
- On February 7, 1998 ABC's Michael McQueen said, "'The question now is whether Starr's tactics will prove more offensive to the courts and the public than any alleged wrongdoing by the President that Starr is investigating.'" ("Ken Starr Gets His Day; Media Had All year").

The above were just some of the sharp criticism Starr received from the supposedly objective media. Democrats alleged Starr was partisan and the media jumped all over the story. The media constantly bought the Democrats' complaints and stirred up public support against Starr. The constant Starr bashing people heard on network television brainwashed some into thinking that Starr was evil and Clinton was the victim. Note this was the same basic strategy used in the other scandals, only now the stakes were upgraded to the prosecutor, himself. It was truly unprecedented.

From the beginning of his appointment, Starr became a problem to the Clintons and thus a major nuisance for the liberal media.

Hence, this "nonpartisan" media did what they could to discredit Starr and save Clinton.

The networks used slanted coverage of Starr's indictment of Hubbell for not paying taxes to further debase Starr. Federal Judge James Robertson threw out the indictment against Hubbell. ABC's "World News Tonight," "CBS Evening News," and CNN's "The World Today" began their shows with stories on the judge's decision. NBC also mentioned the story. The morning shows gave the news substantial coverage. "Good Morning America," "This Morning," and "Today" mentioned the new development. These programs did not just report but stressed Starr was an overreaching prosecutor. ABC's Jackie Judd "reported" that the news hurt "'Starr's image as a man of justice'," and CNN's John King explored how the decision yielded "'new questions about the independent counsel and his hardball tactics'" ("The Wild Swings in Hubbell's Relevance").

All of the networks and three morning shows the next day mentioned the dismissal of the indictment, but on January 26,1999 when a court reinstated the indictment, the decision drew hardly a whisper. The next day none of the morning news programs mentioned the reinstatement. ABC "World News Tonight" and "NBC Nightly News" both of whom mentioned the dismissal did not mention the federal appeals court's decision to overturn Robertson's ruling. The "CBS Evening News" and CNN's "The World Today' both had found time to air full stories on Robertson's decision, but managed only seconds for coverage on the latest turn in the case ("The Wild Swings in Hubbell's Relevance").

The difference in coverage was not right, but not surprising. The media protected the president that they overwhelmingly supported. Stories that claimed to demonstrate the prosecutor as partisan and doing an unfair job were news, while stories that exonerated Starr indicating he was, in fact, just fulfilling his mandate were apparently not newsworthy. The news should consist of everything significant. If the media during the Clinton presidency had been concerned with informing the public objectively, all sides of issues should have received approximately equal time. But here again with Hubbell this was not the case.

It is interesting to compare the relative media silence when Tripp's indictment was permanently thrown out in Maryland with the temporary dismissal of Hubbell's indictment. Funny how the media questioned Starr's motives in response to the development but not Montanarelli's. Can you guess which party was the beneficiary of this double standard?

Donald Smaltz and the Media

Independent Counsel Donald Smaltz also got a raw deal from the media. As the Espy independent counsel he worked diligently to hold wealthy and powerful people accountable. At the beginning of NBC's news program on Wednesday, December 2, 1998 Tom Brokaw summed the Espy investigation up as "'A stunning verdict in the corruption trial of a former Clinton cabinet member. Another expensive investigation by an independent counsel adds up to nothing'" (Baker, "Dan Rather: Hillary for Chief Justice; Smaltz Empty?: Olbermann's Last Days").

A news anchor's job is to be objective. He or she should allow both sides of an issue to state their opinion and then allow the public to decide for itself. The anchor should not take sides or present one side as the truth, and thus undermine other opinions. Brokaw's comments about the Smaltz investigation did just what an anchor should not do. Two sides existed to the Smaltz investigation. Liberals claimed an excessive investigation wasting taxpayer money. On the other hand, conservatives claimed it was an effective investigation. Although unable to convict Espy, it did lead to fifteen convictions and eleven million dollars in fines (Baker, "Dan Rather: Hillary for Chief Justice; Smaltz Empty?: Olbermann's Last Days"). Brokaw should have presented both sides of the issue. Instead, Brokaw told the subjective liberal spin as fact when really it was just an opinion.

CNBC's Geraldo Rivera also mentioned the "expensive"

investigation and dubbed the allegations "trivial" (Baker, "Dan Rather: Hillary for Chief Justice; Smaltz Empty?: Olbermann's Last Days"). Excuse me, Mr. Rivera, but white collar crime is by no means "trivial." Allegations of bribery, conflicts of interest, obstruction of justice, and perjury are quite serious offenses.

ChinaGate and the Media

ChinaGate was possibly the most serious Clinton scandal and maybe one of the most harmful presidential scandal ever, though the scope of it may not be fully comprehended for years to come. Regardless of possible wrongdoing, the media was reluctant to inform the public about it and was skeptical when they did. They did not lead the search for answers and never elevated it to the level of say, Iran-Contra during the Reagan presidency. To the contrary, the media looked the other way and let the episode pass without kicking up any more dust than absolutely necessary.

During the Clinton presidency, whistle-blowers made important revelations about the ChinaGate scandal that the network media ignored. For example, on June 16, 1998 Bill Gertz of The Washington Times reported China was contemplating selling missile test equipment to Iran and aided Libya's missile program. This development contrasted with the Clinton administration's report that China "'improved its record on weapons proliferation.'" This story got zero network coverage ("Networks Continue to Ignore news Broken by Newspapers on ChinaGate").

The story, if accurate, was significant. Was the Clinton administration lying to the public? Who orchestrated the misinformation and for what purpose? The media should have asked these questions and others. They needed to highlight this issue because misrepresentation to the public especially about national security issues is unacceptable. The country needed answers, none were forthcoming. Rather than properly informing and searching for the truth, again the media could care less.

Another largely missed ChinaGate development was Johnny

Chung's testimony that the leader of Chinese military intelligence was the origin of $300,000 Chung received to donate to Democrats. Two weeks after this revelation, "CBS Evening News," MSNBC's "The News with Brian Williams," ABC's "Good Morning America," and NBC's "Today" still hadn't mentioned the development (Baker, "Reno as victim; Clinton is on cover up?; McCarthyite Republicans"). Whatever the media's agenda, they were not picking up this ball and running with it. I am certainly curious: if Chung's testimony is accurate, why was such a source of funds going to a major U.S. political party? Maybe Katie Couric and the others concluded curiosity killed the cat.

Chung also alleged DNC officials knowingly accepted this illegal Chinese money. Instead of giving the allegations major coverage, the media basically looked the other way. CNN did one story and CBS ran one nineteen second piece but that was it. NBC and ABC refused to inform the public. ("Networks Continue to Ignore news Broken by Newspapers on ChinaGate").

Another central figure in the ChinaGate scandal was John Huang. Although allegedly immersed in the scandal, the media largely avoided Huang and his revelations. On October 27, 1999 John Huang's statements to the FBI were released implicating Harold Ickes, a former top Clinton aide who was then running Hillary Clinton's U.S. Senate campaign, of pressuring Huang to contribute money to Jesse Jackson Jr.'s Congressional campaign. The next day, The Washington Post published a story about the case. However, the evening news programs that day on ABC, CNN, MSNBC, and NBC all ignored the alleged illegal actions of a close Clinton confidant. Only Fox News aired a full story. CBS briefly mentioned the allegation in a twenty-six second blurb, but Dan Rather sounded more like a member of Clinton's damage control team than an objective news anchor (Baker, "Zilch on ABC, CNN & NBC on Huang/Riady Revelations; Helms' Women Problem"). Rather said, "'House Republicans…also want to ask Huang about allegations that Harold Ickes, a longtime Clinton family friend and effective aide, asked Huang to carry out what the Republicans say were questionable fundraising tactics'" (Baker, "Zilch on ABC, CNN & NBC on Huang/Riady Revelations; Helms' Women problem").

That statement was less than objective. Dan Rather subtly defended the Clintons and made the investigation seem partisan. However, it was not true because according to The Washington Post, Republicans did not decide Ickes alleged actions were suspicious but United States statutory law did. It is illegal for government officials to solicit contributions from lower ranked employees. (Baker, "Zilch on ABC, CNN & NBC on Huang/Riady Revelations; Helms' Women Problem"). That fact was of little moment to the star anchor. Rather's word choice was no accident. They expressed his disdain for the investigation into a Democrat.

The media often referred to the obligation to investigate Clinton as "politics." They could just as well have called it "politics" when the Democrats repeatedly ignored evidence of malfeasance and objected to these investigations. Of course, that was not the message they wanted to put forth.

The media refused to do its job. Bill Clinton should have been asked, "'How has this damaged your presidency?'" and "'How can you not know?'" He should have been asked, "'Doesn't it look suspicious?'" after all the money they gave you, and "'Why don't you just come clean and be done with it?'" (Baker, "Gun Control Before Espionage at CBS & NBC, More Time for Wrestling in the AM").

The media asked those questions of President Ronald Reagan in just one press conference. The media rightfully granted significant coverage to the Iran-Contra scandal. Entire newscasts were devoted to it. Dan Rather grilled Vice President George Bush about the scandal on television, but did Rather even bother to bring up ChinaGate in his March 31, 1999 interview with Clinton? Of course not (Baker, "Gun Control Before Espionage at CBS & NBC, More Time for Wrestling in the AM").

The media's coverage of ChinaGate gives the impression the media is not that concerned with political scandals. Yet, that is not always true. It often depends on your political affiliation.

When the media did give a little attention to the ChinaGate scandal, the type of coverage they gave differed greatly from the Iran-Contra affair. In the latter case, the media constantly questioned the authority and sought the truth. In ChinaGate the media did its best to dismiss the allegations and to obfuscate the truth. The media immediately dubbed allegations as politics and expressed cynicism toward the allegations. For example, rather than investigating, NBC's "Today" co-host Katie Couric did her best to put the scandal to rest when she said, "'Isn't there a possibility that China could have done this (improved its nuclear warheads) on its own (without spying)?'" (Baker, "Gun Control Before Espionage at CBS & NBC, More Time for Wrestling in the AM"). Few of the media elites cut the Reagan administration any slack in the Iran-Contra situation, but with Clinton and you name the scandal, the beat goes on (Baker, "Gun Control Before Espionage at CBS & NBC, More Time for Wrestling in the AM"). No wonder there is so much cynicism today among young people.

So what happened to the investigative media? Did they die? No, I guess they were hibernating, setting the alarm for the new Republican administration, no doubt. They will then wake up and courageously do their job once again. We probably won't hear too much about "politics," "costs" of investigations, or the accuser's motives either.

EmailGate and the Media

EmailGate involved a possible malfeasance and cover up. It was either a malicious attempt to hide subpoenaed emails or an honest mistake that prevented the recording of controversial emails. The media seemed willing to accept the administration's explanation deeming the problem a glitch. They did not give the scandal much attention. As a consequence the media did not question or search for the truth, differing substantially from their response to the Watergate tape gap twenty-five years earlier.

On Thursday March 23, 2000 the House Government Reform

Committee probed the White House email problem, and on that day the Justice Department announced an investigation. The next day even the left leaning The Washington Post and The New York Times thought the story was front-page material, but apparently the morning shows did not. NBC and CBS both granted the new developments zero coverage while ABC allotted the scandal a short seventeen seconds. Even in this piece the station emphasized "Republicans" were making charges, not career government workers (Baker, "E-mail Bounced by Nets; ABC's Clinton Retraction, Shriver's Edelman Glorification").

One of the key whistle-blowers in the scandal, Sheryl Hall, a career federal worker in charge of the White House's computer and phone systems, believed that Hillary Clinton's office plotted to conceal emails from investigators. Hall interviewed with ABC and CNN. However, after three weeks the interviews still had not aired. Around that time an anonymous network employee source told her the station vetoed it (Sperry, "CNN, ABC spike reports after taping interviews with e-mail whistle-blower").

ABC and CNN got a good story from Sheryl Hall, possibly too good. Hall had credibility which automatically made her a threat to the administration. Rather than airing her story and letting the public decide for themselves, the media canceled it, insuring the public bought the White House's spin.

The media barely covered the story. According to numerous credible witnesses with nothing to gain, EmailGate was a deliberate attempt to obstruct justice, plain and simple. The media should have aired those credible allegations and sought the truth. If the media had done that, the public would have responded pressuring Congress and the Justice Department to get serious about executive malfeasance. Again, the mainstream media did not report, leaving most of the public unaware of the issue, so it drifted off to oblivion.

I find it curious that the media elites and their liberal friends are universally supportive of whistle-blowers who leak top secret security defense documents or expose the purchase of $800 toilet seats but had to be pulled kicking and screaming just to cover claims against the Clintons, let alone fair and balanced. If the allegation is an assault on the sucker fish or too many picnic lunches carelessly tossed in the Hudson River, they are all over the story. But if the charge was a sitting president undermining the bedrock of our legal system by lying under oath, it was reduced to a private matter between consenting adults, not much to be concerned with. Whether the issue was only a few hundred thousand emails or hundreds of FBI files or several state troopers pimping for the executive, ditto, ditto, ditto! It all depends on whose ox is gored, I guess. If it is a liberal at risk, guess whose gone fishing?

TrooperGate and the Media

The media also basically ignored the TrooperGate scandal. When the TrooperGate story broke in the end of 1993 ABC did not invite David Brock or R. Emmett Tyrrell of The American Spectator to discuss the scandal. The network never invited the Arkansas State troopers to inform the public about their allegation either. It seems ABC has a double standard, ABC would not let people air allegations about a liberal president, but the station readily invited reporters Jil Abramson and Jane Mayer to discuss their book based on allegations about Clarence Thomas (Graham, "ABC: Larry Flynt's Outreach Partner"). Parenthetically, once a more "enlightened" David Brock mystically converted politically, his reportings mysteriously became more newsworthy, despite by his own acknowledgment that his credibility now is suspect. I bet those cocktail party invitations have also been rolling in.

ABC was so eager to suppress the story that it rejected airing a piece that veteran reporter Jim Wooten did on the TrooperGate episode. According to ABC sources, ABC pulled it after the White House groused to Wooten's boss, Rich Kaplan, a Clinton friend (Powers, "Media Rex: Scandal-Shy").

ABC's job as a news station is to provide the public with the facts. Censoring stories detrimental to President Clinton is not ABC's job. ABC should have presented the public with the facts and let the public decide. Instead, ABC acted in a totalitarian manner and decided what the public should or should not know for essentially political reasons, which I believe is an abuse of its discretion.

The other news networks should have exploited ABC's reluctance to air the scandal in order to expand their viewing base, but instead they basically performed similar stunts. All of the network news stations combined only gave the scandal a mere twenty-two stories in twelve days after the revelation (Graham, "Media Should Say Whoops Over Whoopee").

The media was not serious about the TrooperGate scandal. Yes, I understand that all news outlets everyday have to make judgments about what gets reported and in what depth. But was there a trend here? At some point, take your pick where, shouldn't it have dawned on some media elites maybe the Clintons do not deserve the benefit of the doubt. Moreover, maybe there was some fatal flaw in the character of our leadership. Once again the wrong lesson went out, especially to my generation. It was getting like the old days in the Wild West where anything goes, well, at least in the Clinton White House.

FileGate and the Media

The media did not completely censor FileGate but did basically suppress some of the biggest revelations in the scandal. For example, on July 25, 1996 Rep. William Clinger claimed a FBI agent's notes after an interview with then White House Counsel Bernard Nussbaum, contradicted Hillary Clinton and showed she arranged the hiring of Craig Livingstone. Although the story indicated the First Lady was hiding something, only ABC aired the story ("TV's Top Ten Undercovered Stories").

At the very least, the mass media should have aired the latest development, so the public could have learned the news, but only ABC did. The media should have pursued the truth by constantly questioning Hillary Clinton and her cohorts: why are you lying, what are you covering up, and why don't you just tell the truth? Media exposure would have stirred up public momentum leading to some answers. It might have made it easier for the independent counsel to do his job and created enough pressure for someone to talk. However, the media did not do this. No one talked and the scandal slipped by with no accountability. It defies credibility. The media did not care. The Justice Department was out to lunch, and Congress was impotent divided basically along party lines on all these scandals. Was anyone watching the store?

Another breakthrough in the FileGate scandal happened on September 25, 1996 when Senator Orinn Hatch divulged a six month gap in the log listing who accessed the FBI files. On October 4, 1996, Hatch released the deposition of White House aide Mari Anderson who confirmed the gap and claimed that Livingstone and others knew the FBI files were of Republicans ("TV's Top Ten Undercovered Stories").

The revelations indicated a cover up. The Hatch revelations showed that the White House possibly destroyed the records so the public would not know who accessed the files. The revelations also demonstrated the White House might have lied about the possession of the files being an honest error. What is the Clinton administration hiding? What is the administration doing with private FBI files? The Clinton administration's lack of respect for the public was unacceptable, as is the media's lackadaisical approach to each and every Clinton scandal.

For starters the media barely informed the public or questioned the principals. Only CNN reported both days of the Hatch revelations. The only network to air the new Hatch revelations was a single brief piece on "Good Morning America" ("TV's Top Ten Undercovered Stories").

Unauthorized access to FBI files is a criminal offense. Yet again, White House big wigs were not held accountable at the expense of justice and respect for our laws. The media's stonewall was so complete that no one ever even had to admit who hired Craig Livingstone. It is preposterous. It is as if I could just walk in the White House sit at a desk and obtain FBI files with a phone call. What an example this is for the young people of this country!

Hubbell Hush Money and the Media

The media certainly did not care about apparent hush money either. When Webster Hubbell was in a position to give evidence against the Clintons, he received significant amounts of money either given or solicited by Clinton associates. Just those two facts would make one suspicious of a possible money-for-silence understanding. You don't have to be a federal prosecutor; it's just common sense. The media being a public watchdog should have asked questions, explored the facts, and thoroughly investigated the issue. Yet, the media refrained from doing this and virtually ignored that aspect of the scandal.

On February 24, 1997 Webster Hubbell failed to assist with the House and Senate questions. CBS and NBC evening news shows gave the story a mere two sentences each. While ABC and the morning shows ignored Hubbell's refusal to cooperate ("Hush Little Hubbell, Don't You Cry"). This is important because Hubbell's plea agreement required his cooperation.

Why is Hubbell not cooperating? What is he hiding? Those were two questions the media should have asked. The important story should have gotten substantial coverage on all the networks, but of course it did not. Once again the media chose not to lead on the story. Instead, the media followed it tepidly until it petered out.

On March 6, 1997 The New York Times reported that Hubbell profited $400,000 from companies, including money from Lippo, the multibillion dollar Chinese company. CBS did a story on it but shunned the China factor while ABC and NBC decided not to report it at all ("Hush Little Hubbell, Don't You Cry").

Then on April 16, 1997 Susan Schmidt of The Washington Post reported that Webster Hubbell met with administration aides over seventy times between his resignation and plea bargain. The story got zero network coverage ("Hush Little Hubbell, Don't You Cry").

Hubbell stayed in contact with the Clinton administration, received money from those associated with the administration, and did not cooperate with authorities. These three facts seem connected.

Normally the media would connect the dots or at the very least report it. The facts were so blatantly obvious. No expensive investigation was necessary. All the media had to do was report, but even that was expecting too much. An uninformed electorate would never be able to make the association.

The Clintons claimed they lacked knowledge of Hubbell's improprieties in 1994, but an old memo surfaced informing Hillary Clinton that the RTC was investigating Hubbell. Another Clinton inconsistency surfaced on May 3, 1997 when The Washington Post revealed that the Clintons met with Hubbell in 1994 more times than previously admitted. Both errors got zero network coverage ("Hush Little Hubbell, Don't You Cry"). The networks should have played these misstatements up or at the very least reported them.

Does anyone doubt that the media would have been so reticent in these matters if the inhabitant was a conservative Republican—actually any Republican, dead or alive? There may be a life's lesson in all of this for America's young, but it unfortunately is not that crime does not pay.

Summary

The media's job is to bring the public the truth through objective reporting, editorializing should be clearly identified. The media uses many tactics including interviews, investigations, airing stories, and simply reporting the news. Normally the media does this, but not so thoroughly with the Clintons. The mainstream television media's actions helped the Clintons escape responsibility. Evidence and allegations were ignored. Questions were either not asked or were not the tough one's that needed to be answered. Liberal spin was spread as fact. The major media did whatever they could to help the Clintons. Although the networks will not admit it, they clearly used a different standard of coverage for the Clintons as compared to Republican leaders and Clinton whistle-blowers.

Remember with the Broadderick allegation, NBC was so worried about checking sources. The station had four verifying witnesses but still wanted more. It wanted to make sure it did not spread falsehoods. Well with other stories, such as Mayer accusing Tripp of lying on her security form, the media did not exert the same precaution. There was no talk about checking sources or factual journalism. The networks all rushed to air the allegation.

With examples like these it is hard to understand how people can question liberal media bias. Yet, many do. Often times these people attempt to take the offensive and bring up conservative talk radio. It is true the majority of renowned talk show hosts are conservative. But this is a case of comparing apples to oranges. For starters, with the exception of Rush Limbaugh, talk show audiences are small and lack the influence of the network news shows. The main difference, however, is the word "news." The talk show hosts do not claim to spread objective fact but spread an agenda through their analysis. They do not mask their conservative ideology. If Dan Rather called his show "From the Left" or another appropriate accolade highlighting his agenda, no problem would arise. It is a misnomer to call these programs "news." They should be identified as broadcast spin intended to promote a left leaning agenda. Let's call a spade a spade.

Media bias significantly helped the Clintons. The Clintons' best spin defense dubbed the allegations a bunch of right wing lies from Clinton bashers. This defense worked because the media did not report to the contrary. Thus, the public was uninformed and accepted the defense that no merit existed, just those crazy Republicans playing politics and trying to spread their hatred of Clinton. The majority of people depend on the network news to report the news, but the networks sure fell short when it came to the Clintons' scandals. Most people don't have the time or inclination to research the available information, so they trusted the Dan Rathers of the world.

The net result was the media aided the Clintons at the expense of young people. The media allowed the Clintons to get away with doing wrong, covering up, being inconsistent, lying, using "personal destruction," and not taking responsibility. The media's lack of reporting the inappropriateness of the reprehensible behavior told children it was not wrong.

Part Four Conclusion

Growing up children read excellent novels such as <u>1984</u> and <u>Fahrenheit 451</u>. Both are about totalitarian governments where new ideas are censored. People are not allowed to think for themselves and are punished if they challenge the government or Big Brother. When these books are read, the children are young and idealistic. They rightfully scorn the ideology. These children have heard "democracy," "freedom of speech," and "freedom of thought" associated with our government and are grateful to live in the United States of America.

However, are Oceania of <u>1984</u> and the United States becoming alike? In our country, the government is yet to raise children, but a political philosophy does. These children go to schools where liberal teachers teach them. They listen to liberal news programs where opinions are presented as fact. As adults, they are free to do what they want. However, if they claim unwanted sexual advances with the president, they may get audited. If they inform about corruption, they may be indicted or have their privacy violated. Is this the way of a democracy? This is one question young people do not want to hear. Their naiveté causes them to think everything will be as advertised. Is it?

Part Five
Wrap Up

Chapter 13
Fool Me Once Shame on You, Fool me twice, Shame on Me

At a young age I learned the proverb, fool me once shame on you, fool me twice shame on me. My parents explained that the saying means you should learn from your mistakes. No one is perfect. Everyone makes mistakes. The difference between success and failure is often the ability to learn from those mistakes. It is acceptable to make a mistake, but do not repeat the same error.

Obviously, this applied to the Clintons, but what has been learned from the experience? I have compiled the Clintons' record of sleaze, their pushing the envelope to the outer fringes, and their wrongdoing from Arkansas to Washington. Were those who supported Clinton duped or simply taken in by his charm, intelligence, and slick talk? Were they seduced by a job and a strong economy? Did they prostitute the values and ethics they were teaching their young for that pay check while ignoring the barrage of disturbing allegations and the unending layers of scandal?

I believe that ultimately it is the children, the family, and indeed the very fabric of our society that has suffered from enduring and tolerating the Clinton years. For children the waters were muddied as to right and wrong. It was a time that exposed the hypocrisy of parental guidance: demonstrating compromised values, do as I say, not as I do. Clinton did just about everything that a parent would advise against. He lied, covered up, verbally attacked those perceived as a threat, was disloyal to friends, and basically only cared about himself. Clinton had a "'You got to do what you gotta do'" ("the New Senate Politics") attitude that superseded all other interests.

President Clinton is out of power now, so what's the difference one might inquire? To ask the question is to have missed the point. It is the future I am concerned about, not the past, and the imprint embedded in the nation's conscience. People learn best by example and practice, and children are the most susceptible of all. These children observed a spectrum of disgraceful conduct from a sitting president committing perjury without punishment to repeated declarations that oral sex was somehow not sex. The danger is that they will try to emulate the Clintons' strategies while lacking the power, communication skills, and support system of their mentor. Those who follow the Clintons' model undoubtedly are in for a rude awakening.

Hopefully the Clinton presidency will prove to be an anomaly, not a precedent for politicians and others in positions of trust and power. Frankly, I have my doubts. As long as the tactics work, there are those who will try to exploit them. Character assassinations worked for Clinton and his acolytes, so we saw Governor Gray Davis attacking the management of Texas utility companies for the California energy problems, conveniently ignoring conservationist and environmental policies that thwarted production for many years. When the personal and financial dealings of Rev. Jesse Jackson were questioned, rather than addressing the issue directly, which should be the obligation of any public figure using tax exempt donations, there was an attack on the motives of the messenger, Bill O'Reilly. Whether it is a senator facing allegations of bribery or a congressman's involvement in a liaison or worse, the response follows a pattern: hire a legal team, hold on to power at all costs, stonewall, obfuscate, demean the accuser or the victim. Sound familiar?

The Clinton era has created a heightened level of cynicism. Many question and even distrust their democratically elected government. When missing FBI documents suddenly appeared, immediately after FBI Director Freeh announced his resignation, and shortly before the scheduled McVeigh execution, there were those I am sure who wondered, honest mistake or a page out of the Clinton play book—read Hillary's billing records. This skepticism can lead to a diminution of confidence in our institutions of government and that is not a healthy situation for any of us.

I believe character, values, morals do matter for all of us, and especially in our political leaders who enjoy great power and influence. If one can not be responsible in the most interpersonal relationships, how can there be trust among constituents and professional associates? Furthermore, it does not suffice to simply say Clinton was too shrewd or blame a complicitous Justice Department or a largely adoring media. To paraphrase Shakespeare, the fault lies with us.

This is not a liberal-conservative, Democrat-Republican issue. It transcends labels. All participants should hold their candidates and leaders to the highest standards. This should be a prerequisite. If the parties fail to do so, the public should reject them. There are well qualified, honest, articulate individuals representing all philosophies. Why must we settle for less? Yet having said all this, we see Hillary Clinton elected United States Senator from New York of all places. Surely there are distinguished New York Democrats with respected records and value systems who could better and more honorably represent the Empire State.

What does it all mean? Has the United States fallen into a hopeless morass or were the Clinton years a freak of nature with the sun, moon, and stars aligning in a once in an eternity pattern? I do not know much about astrology but as a seventeen year old looking toward the future, there has to be a positive side to these events. Lincoln said, "It is true that you may fool all the people some of the time; you can even fool some of the people all the time; but you can't fool all of the people all the time." It should be noted that Clinton never won a majority of the votes cast in either the 1992 or 1996 election. When first elected president, Democrats controlled both Houses of Congress and thirty governorships. When he left office in January 2001 Republicans recaptured the presidency, narrowly controlled both Houses of Congress, and held thirty governorships. Furthermore, despite high job approval ratings, even during the impeachment period, he left office with the majority of those polled believing he is a person of low moral character and integrity. Finally, whether a supporter of Mr. Clinton or not, I find it hard to believe that anyone can look in the mirror, or send a child to the military or off to school or even out on a date when he was president and express pride and respect in our forty-second president's behavior.

Chapter 14
Me Again

The spring and summer of 2001, marked the first time in ten or more seasons that I did not try out and play on a baseball team. I love the game, but I wanted to finish this manuscript before college commenced in the fall. I know that assorted professional experts have covered the Clintons' scandals ad nauseam over the years, yet I still believed there was something to add from a young person's perspective. I believe the Clinton phenomenon has left deep scars on the soul of American life. Particularly effected are the young who saw parents turn a blind eye to the endless stream of scandals and malfeasance, who preached lofty goals and values but fell short themselves. I wrote this book to address this perceived dichotomy and its likely consequences. Adults, who clearly would not want this philanderer for a spouse, or depend on him as a friend, or leave him five minutes with their daughter, or trust him with their legitimate business interests, apparently concluded that for a president he was okay.

It saddens me that parents still do not get it. Children see the president as a role model who should set the highest moral and ethical standards, values to which we all can aspire. If you do not want your kids to behave irresponsibly, to lie, and deceive, then do not rationalize that a president's disgraceful actions are somehow acceptable. In today's vernacular, you have to talk the talk and walk the walk. Nothing is a bigger turn off to a kid than this do as I say, not as I do mentality.

Some people may dismiss this analysis as just that of another Clinton basher. I refuse to be put on the defensive. I believe the office of the presidency was debased and the public trust violated by Mr. Clinton. It is a further shame that Clinton himself, an obviously bright man with a golden tongue, diminished his own legacy by his personal failings.

I consider myself a compassionate young person with no political agenda or ax to grind while growing up in the 1990's. I think in the fullness of time, sociologists will study and debate the ramifications of issues raised herein. America is a great nation with a heritage that is the envy of the world. People often try not to be too judgmental. But there are times when events require a judgment, when a sophisticated society must definitively declare something right or wrong. It is my contention that at some point during the Clinton years, Americans unambiguously should have said, " enough…we will tolerate this no more." Time will tell.

EPILOGUE

Much has transpired in the world since I saved the completed manuscript on my computer hard drive and went off to college, simultaneously facing academic challenges while seeking a publisher. As always in life some events were unforeseeable, even unthinkable, other occurrences were more predictable and mundane. In little over a year the nation experienced everything from catastrophic terrorism at home, to a military mobilization for a war abroad, to unprecedented instances of corporate corruption by some of America's titans of industry with considerable congressional chatter about executives going to jail. Yet other matters on the world stage seem strangely unaffected despite these calamitous happenings.

Question: Name a recent, well-known CEO who ascended to the job despite a history of self-dealing which engulfed him in accusations of corruption, who from his first days of employment was surrounded by scandal, some old, some new, covering the gambit from sexual harassment in the workplace, suicide of an associate, felony convictions of colleagues, to lying under oath. He was indicted during his tenure but lacked the decency to step down. He is a man who had publicized liaisons at the office while enemies of his organization were planning its destruction; one who even stole the furniture when he finally left his position and for good measure facilitated the release of some evil people from jail, arguably in exchange for donations to his favorite charity. Yet he maintains the confidence of those he served and even today is admired as a celebrity wherever he goes, commanding upwards of two hundred fifty thousand dollars for a speech and millions of dollars for his memoirs.

Of course it is the forty-second President of the United States, William Jefferson Clinton, the Teflon President. To my mind the fast and loose style that characterized his anything goes tenure is largely responsible for many challenges this country faces today.

I know what you're thinking: "Here he goes again. Despite being out of office everything bad is still Clinton's fault. Get over it." Well, hear me out. Let us connect the dots to understand what has happened to our country. I am not claiming an absolute cause and effect, but Clinton did indeed create an atmosphere in which negative repercussions were destined to reverberate throughout the entire spectrum of life's activities. A leader with no shame and no standards except "what's best for me at any cost." His scandals are legion. For the children he proclaimed oral sex is not sex. For the adults he demonstrated that one could slip through any conundrum, if slick enough, deceitful enough, and willing to expend whatever capital it took to prevail. Houdini would have been impressed.

Many people of wealth and power have recently been implicated in shameful behavior. Their shenanigans are crucifying the average working person. Jobs are being lost that are difficult to replace. College funds and company retirement plans are being wiped out at an alarming rate. These abuses currently being uncovered were conceived and nurtured during the excesses of the freewheeling 1990's, the Clinton years. Why did so many formerly reputable executives push the envelope over the edge and engage in illicit business practices? Many experts postulate that one explanation for the explosion of improprieties is greed. Other pundits believe stock options, originally designed to encourage executives to invest in their companies, are the culprits. No doubt there is some truth in these analyses.

The myriad of business transgressions, however, suggests a sea change in thinking, a moral compass run amuck. Some evidently have erroneously concluded that there are no boundaries. They have everything but still want more. They believe they can befuddle the public, the authorities, and exploit the system with impunity.

I believe these patterns were at the very least accelerated when the self-proclaimed "most ethical administration" entered the White House on January 20, 1993. Of course the Clinton administration was anything but moral and quickly became immersed in never ending scandals. However, the Clintons were always able to use their wits and power to evade responsibility. The message sent and the lesson learned was that the powerful can wrong and walk away unscathed. A politicized Justice Department reinforced the perception. Obfuscation, bungling, or simply caving in to the powerful and well-connected became the norm as exemplified by numerous lax prosecutions. This may have contributed to a relaxing of ethics and moral decay amongst some business elite. It is only logical for some to have rationalized that if Clinton could wrong and not only survive, but flourish, why can't they? If the President of the United States can lie to the American people, then why can't a CEO prevaricate to the shareholders? After all, the president is ultimately responsible for the entire economy not just a single business empire. It should be no surprise that we are in an environment of rampant corruption. The primary deterrent to crime and abuse of power is punishment and rebuke, but the Clinton travails were ameliorated by a duplicitous Department of Justice and an accommodating media.

From these occurrences society must also understand the theory of trickle down morality. People learn acceptable behavior from their superiors: parents, teachers, employers, and yes, political leaders. As one progresses up the social hierarchy, one's actions have a broader influence. Thus we must hold those who have reached the top to the highest standards. If the public can accept this, perhaps some good will come from this sorry chapter in our history.

While we are connecting the dots, it is important to keep President Clinton in perspective. He is not a lovable rogue, not a Professor Harold Hill-like character from the Broadway musical *Music Man*. Rather he is a flawed leader whose shortcomings will continue to have a profound effect on many aspects of our society for years to come.

Perhaps on a subconscious level many people easily accepted a president with such obvious character defects because it made them feel better about their own foibles, but in their hearts they knew it wasn't right. Though the impeached president served out his term, he sullied the Office and betrayed the trust of those who believed in him. It is understandable he would want to resurrect his legacy, but I do take umbrage at this man who lied under oath, pardoned terrorists, and coped a plea to avoid prosecution in the final hours of his presidency. I believe he departed in disgrace and history will so record. Whether Bill Clinton was a product of a society in decline, or merely a proponent, or the primary propagator of moral and ethical decay is a debate in which historians have yet to write the final chapter.

BIBLIOGRAPHY

"Actress Who Claimed Sex with Bill Says IRS is Hounding her," *New York Post*, [Online] Available http://home.hiwaay.net~craigg/g4c/gracen.htm, (19 May 2001)

"Address to the Nation on Testimony Before the Independent Counsel's Grand Jury," 17 August 1998, [Online] Available http://www.lib.umich.edu/libhome/Documents.center/text/aug1798.txt, (9 April 2001)

"Amended Complaint," http://209.70.190.2/cases/browning/browning2.htm, (12 May 2001)

Anderson, Ben, "Burton Calls for Special Counsel on Missing White House Email," 27 March 2000, [Online] Available http://usconservatives.about.com/newsissues/usconservatives/bln0327email.htm, (14 February 2001)

Anderson, Kerby, "It Takes a Village An Analysis of Hillary Clinton's Book," 2 September 2000, [Online] Available http://www.leaderu.com/orgs/probe/docs/village.html, (2 February 2001)

Associated Press, "Chung sentenced for illegal contributions," *USA Today*, 1999, [Online] Available http://www.usatoday.com/news/index/finance/ncfin338.htm, (27 May 2001)

Associated Press, "Clinton had fundraising breakfasts in '94," *USA Today*, 25 September1997, [Online] Available http://www.usatoday.com/news/index/finance/ncfin107.htm, (26 February 2001)

Associated Press, "Democratic fund-raiser pleads guilty," *USA Today*, 1999, [Online] Available http://www.usatoday.com/news/index/finance/ncfin255.htm, (27 May 2001)

Associated Press, "Ickes reportedly told of Clinton calls from White House," *USA today*, 26 September 1997, [Online] Available http://www.usatoday.com/news/index/finance/ncfin110.htm, (26 February 2001)

Associated Press, "Independent Counsel: Hillary Clinton Gave 'Inaccurate' TravelGate Testimony," *Fox News*, 18 October 2000, [Online] Available http://www.foxnews.com/elections/101800/travelgate.sml, (5 February 2001)

Associated Press, "Linda Tripp Fired From Pentagon Job," *LA Times*, 19 January 2001, [Online] Available http://www.latimes.com/news/politics/natpol/ap_tripp010119.htm, (9 May 2001)

Associated Press, "Tripp indicted for wiretapping in Maryland," *CNN All Politics*, 30 July 1999, [Online] Available http://www.cnn.com/ALLPOLITICS/stories/1999/07/30/linda.tripp/, (11 June 2001)

Associated Press, "Witness: White House sold trips for funds," *USA Today*, 1999, [Online] Available http://www.usatoady.com/news/index/finance/ncfin259.htm, (29 May 2001)

"Author of "Unlimited Access" Says Hillary hired FileGate figure, Craig Livingstone," *Reagan Information Interchange*, 2 July 1996, [Online] Available http://reagan.com/HotTopics.main/Hot Mike/document-7.2.1996.2.html, (12 April 2001)

Baker, Brent, "CBS Bought Hillary's 'Candor'; $90,000 Skipped in AM; 'Stupid Tax Cut'," *Media Research Center*, 2 August 1999, [Online] Available http://www.mediaresearch.org/news/cyberalert/1999/cyb19990802.html, (27 June 2001)

Baker, Brent, "Dan Rather: Hillary for Chief Justice; Smaltz Empty?: Olbermann's Last Days," *Media Research Center*, 4 December 1998, [Online] Available http://www.mediaresearch.org/news/cyberalert/1998/cyb19981204.html, (1 July 2001)

Baker, Brent, "E-mail Bounced by Nets; ABC's Clinton Retraction, Shriver's Edelman Glorification," *Media Research Center*, 27 March 2000, [Online] Available http://www.mrc.org/news/cyberalert/2000/cyb20000327.html, (21 June 2001)

Baker, Brent, "Gun Control Before Espionage at CBS & NBC; More Time for Wrestling in the AM," *Media Research Center*, 26 May 1999, [Online] Available http://www.mediaresearch.org/news/cyberalert/1999/cyb19990526.html, (20 June 2001)

Baker, Brent, "Reno as Victim; Clinton in on Cover Up?; McCarthyite Republicans," *Media Research Center*, 25 May 1999, [Online] Available http://www.mrc.org/news/cyberalert/1999/cyb19990525.html, (27 June 2001)

Baker, Brent, "Seconds for Clinton's "Criminal Violation"; Ruling Buried at Press Conference, *Media Research Center*,30 March 2000, [Online] Available http://www.mediaresearch.org/news/cyberalert/2000/cyb20000330.html, (21 June 2001)

Baker, Brent, "Tripp Trumped; Corroboration for Freeh Skipped; Erbe; Expect 'Conservatives to Lie'," *Media Research Center*, 25 May 2000, [Online] Available http://www.mediaresearchcenter.org/news/cyberalert/2000/cyb20000525.html, (27 June 2001)

Baker, Brent, "Willey's Weak Credibility?; Flowers Found; Emma Thompson; Yes to Clinton," *Media Research Center*, 17 March 1998, [Online] Available http://www.mediaresearch.org/news/cyberalert/1998/cyb19980317.html, (21 June 2001)

Baker, Brent, "Zilch on ABC, CNN & NBC on Huang/Riady Revelations; Helms' Women Problem," *Media Research Center*, 29 October 1999, [Online] Available http://www.mediaresearch.org/news/cyberalert/1999/cyb19991029.html, (21 June 2001)

Baker, Peter and Susan Schmidt, "President Had Big Role in Setting Donor Perks," *Washington Post*, 26 February 1997, [Online] Available http://washingtonpost.com/wp-srv/politics/special/campfin/stories/lincoln.htm (26 February 2001)

Barringer, Felicity, and David Firestone, "On Tortuous Route, Sexual Assault Accusation Against Clinton Resurfaces," *New York Times*, 24 February 1999, [Online] Available http://www.shamema.com/nytbroad.htm, (16 February 2001)

Bellafante, Ginia, "The Lives of Kathleen Willey," *Time*, 30 March 1998, [Online] Available http://www.time.com/time/magazine/1998/dom/980330/nation.the_lives_of_kath4.html, (19 February 2001)

Blumenfeld, Samuel, "Vince Foster: Lest We Forget," *Ether Zone*, 15 August 2000, [Online] Available http://www.etherzone.com/2000/blum081500.html, (4 March 2001)

Boyer, Peter, and Michael Kirk, "Secrets of an Independent Counsel," *FreeRepublic*, 3 May 2000, [Online] Available http://www.freerepublic.com/forum/a3910f91f0de5.htm, (9 June 2001)

Bozell, L. Brent, "Nothing New On the Clinton Women," 1 June 2000, [Online] Available http://www.cnsnews.com/bozellcolumn/archive/col2000601.asp, (27 June 2001)

Brock, David, "Living With the Clintons Bill's Arkansas bodyguards tell the story the press missed," *American Spectator*, 21 July 1999, [Online] Available http://www.spectator.org/classics/classics194.htm, (8 March 2001)

Burton, Dan, "Burton Rejects Reno's Reasons for Withholding LaBella and Freeh Memos," 3 August 1998, [Online] Available http://www.house.gov/reform/press/98.08.03.a.htm, (12 June 2001)

Burton, Dan, "The Death of Vince Foster," 30 April 1996, [Online] Available http://www.whatreallyhappened.com/RANCHO/POLITICS/FOSTER_COVERUP/hillprints.html, (5 March 2001)

Burton, Dan, "Opening Statement Chairman Dan Burton Committee on Government Reform," 5 August 1999, [Online] Available http://www.house.gov/reform/oversight/finance/hearings/99.08.05/burton.htm, (16 June 2001)

"Campaign Finance Key Player: Johnny Chung," *Washington Post*, 21 May 1998, [Online] Available http://www.washington post.com/wp-srv/politics/special/campfin/players/chung.htm, (27 May 2001)

"Campaign Finance Key Players: The Riady Family," *Washington Post*, 4 March 1998, [Online] Available http://washingtonpost.com/wp-srv/politics/special/campfin/players/riady.htm, (8 February 2001)

"Charlie Trie Pleads Guilty to Federal Campaign Finance Violations," 21 May 1999, [Online] Available http://www.usdoj.gov/opa/pr/1999/May/201crm.htm, (25 May 2001)

"Charlie Trie Recommended for Contempt in Judicial Watch Case," *Reagan Information Interchange*, 12 April 2000, [Online] Available http://reagan.com/HotTopics.main/HotMike/document-4.12.2000.2.html, (25 May 2001)

Clinger Jr., William F., "Statement on the White House Travel Office," *Reagan Information Interchange*, 4 January 1996, http://www.reagan.com/HotTopics.main/HotMike/document-1.8.1996.1.html, (7 February 2001)

"Clinton denies coaching witness; lawyer attacks Starr," *Nando*, 1998, [Online} Available http://www.nando.net/newsroom/nt/206 no1no1n.html, (3 May 2001)

"Clinton Friend Under Scrutiny," *ABC News*, 16 March 1998, [Online} Available http://www.abcnews.go.com/sections/us/Political Nation/landow0316.html, (9 March 2001)

"Clinton Lied to White House Lawyers about Hubbell," 18 April 1997, [Online} Available http://www.opinioninc.com/current/april/041897.html, (31 May 2001)

"Clinton's Flowers Testimony," *Time*, 30 January 1998, [Online} Available http://www.time.com/time/daily/scandal/flowers _test.html, (26 March 2001)

"Conrad Also Tries to Throw 'Monkey Wrench' Into Lamberth's ChinaGate Court Proceeding," *Judicial Watch*, 29 March 2000, [Online} Available http://209.235.49.36/media/preleases/2000/032900.html, (16 June 2000)

Cosby, Rita "Sources: Mrs. Clinton Gave Lincoln Bedroom to Big Donors," *Fox News*, 13 September 2000, [Online} Available http://www.foxnews.com/elections/091300/hillary_fnc.sml, (26 February 2001)

Coulter, Ann, High Crimes and Misdemeanors: The case against Bill Clinton, United States, Regnery Publishing, INC., 1998

"David hale's testimony," *PBS Frontline*, 1998, http://www.pbs.org/wgbh/pages/frontline/shows/arkansas/docs/hale.html, (12 February 2001)

Dougherty, Jon, "Judge: Clinton committed 'criminal violation'," *FreeRepublic*, 30 March 2000, http://www.freerepublic.com/forum/a38c30ff569c7.htm, (18 May 2001)

Dunleavy, Steve "Elizabeth Gracen: I was a victim of Clinton's reign of terror," *New York Post*, [Online} Available http://home.hiwaay.net~craigg/g4c/gracen.htm, (19 May 2001)

"Espy innocent of all charges," *CNN All Politics*, 2 December 1998, [Online} Available http://www.cnn.com/ALLPOLITICS/stories/1998/12/02/espy/, (28 May 2001)

"Evidence in Whitewater Case is Now Firm," *Washington Weekly*, [Online} Available http://www.washington-weekly.com/oct31i/Evidence, (9 February 2001)

"Excerpt From Kathleen Willey's Interview with 60 Minutes," *The Coffee Shop Times*, 16 March 1998, [Online} Available http://www.coffeeshoptimes.com/willey60.html, (19 February 2001)

"FBI Files Flap," *MSNBC*, [Online} Available http://www.msnbc.com/modules/whitewater/ww_fbi.asp, (7 March 2001)

"Former Agriculture Secretary Espy Indicted," *CNN All Politics*, 27 August 1997, [Online} Available http://www.cnn.com/ALLPOLITICS/1997/08/27espy/, (28 May 2001)

Franken, Bob, "McDougal Changing Tune on Clinton-Hale Meeting," *CNN All Politics*, 10 February 1997, http://www.cnn.com/ALLPOLITICS/1997/02/10/whitewater.franken/, (12 February 2001)

Frieden, Terry, "Hatch demands conclusion to Justice probe of Starr," *CNN ALL Politics*, 17 June 1999, [Online] Available http://www.cnn.com/ALLPOLITICS/stories/1999/06/17/starr.probe/, (11 June 2001)

"Friends & relationships," *PBS Frontline*, 1998, [Online] Available http://www.pbs.org/wgbh/pages/frontline/shows/arkansas/etc/friends.htm, (25 May 2001)

"From I am Woman to Who's that Girl?," *MediaWatch*, June 1994, [Online] Available http://www.mediaresearch.org/news/mediawatch/1994/mw19940601stud.html, (30 June 2001)

"Ft. Marcy Park Witness Patrick Knowlton Lawsuit," [Online] Available http://www.aci.net/kalliste/knowlton_lawsuit.htm, (16 May 2001)

Garrett, Major, "Appeals Court to hear arguments in Willey case," *CNN All Politics*, 19 April 2000, [Online] Available http://www.cnn.com/2000/ALLPOLITICS/stories/04/19/clinton.willey/, (15 June 2001)

"Gennifer Flowers Questions-#1," [Online] Available http://www.thecommonman.com/flowers1.html, (27 March 2001)

Gerth, Jeff, "Ex-Clinton Confidant Gets 21 months," *New York Times*, 29 June 1995, [Online] Available http://www.nytimes.com/books/97/12/14/home/062995hubbell.html, (22 May 2001)

Graham, Tim, "ABC: Larry Flynt's Outreach Partner," *Media Reality Check*, 14 January 1999, [Online} Available http://www.mediaresearch.org/news/reality/1999/fax19990114.html, (21 June 2001)

Graham, Tim, "Media Should Say Whoops Over Whoopee," *Media Reality Check*, 29 January 1998, [Online} Available http://www.mediaresearch.org/news/reality/1998/fax19980129.html, (21 June 2001)

Grier, Peter, and James Skip Thurman, "A President's Right to Secrecy," *Christian Science Monitor*, 26 March 1998, [Online} Available http://www.csmonitor.com/durable/1998/03/26/us/us.5.html, (8 April 2001)

Haddigan, Michael, "McDougal Gets 3-Year Term," *Washington Post*, 15 April 1997, [Online} Available http://www.washingtonpost.com/wp-srv/politics/special/whitewater/stories/wwtr970415.html, (25 May 2001)

Haddigan, Michael, "Susan McDougal Gets 2 Years for Fraud Tied to Whitewater," *Washington Post*, 21 August 1996, [Online} Available http://www.washingtonpost.com/wp-srv/politics/special/whitewater/stories/wwtr960821.htm, (25 May 2001)

Haddigan, Michael, "Tucker Sentenced to 4 Years' Probation," *Washington Post*, 20 August 1996, [Online} Available http://www.washingtonpost.com/wp-srv/politics/special/whitewater/stories/wwtr960820.htm, (25 May 2001)

"Hillary Clinton: "I'm Too Important to Testify," *Judicial Watch*, 15 July 1999, [Online} Available http://www.judicialwatch.org/press_release.asp?pr_id=134, (12 April 2001)

"Hillary's Presidential Slip Showing," *Newsmax*, 19 July 2001, [Online] Available http://www.newsmax.com/showinside. shtml?a=2001/7/19/150039, (26 July 2001)

Hunt, Terence, "Saga Continues for Some," *ABC News*, 15 February 1999, [Online] Available http://abcnews.go.com/sections/us/PoliticalNation/pn_impeachment_990214.html, (24 April 2001)

"Hush Little Hubbell, Don't You Cry," *MediaWatch*, June 1997, [Online] Available http://www.mediaresearch.org/news/mediawatch/1997/mw19970601stud.html, (25 June 2001)

"Inside the Clinton White House," February 2000, [Online] Available http://www.nljonline.com/February2000/itcwh.html, (12 April 2001)

"Interview James Carville," *ABC Nightline*, 2000, [Online] Available http://abcnews.go.com/onair/nightline/clintonyears/clinton/interviews/carville.html, (11 April 2001)

"Investigation of the White House Travel Firings and Related Matters," http://www.house.gov/reform/reports/whitch.htm, (7 February 2001)

"James McDougal On CNN's Larry King Live," *CNN All Politics*, 21 April 1997, [Online] Available http://www.cnn.com/ALLPOLITICS/1997/04/22/fdch/, (31 May 2001)

"James Riady Pleads Guilty Will Pay Largest Fine in Campaign Finance History For Violating Federal Election Law," 11 January 2001, [Online] Available http://www.usdoj.gov/opa/pr/2001/January/017crm.htm, (27 May 2001)

"Jim Guy Tucker, James McDougal-Guilty of Fraud and Conspiracy," *Reagan Information Interchange*, 29 May 1996, [Online] Available http://reagan.com/HotTopics.main/HotMike/document-5.29.1996.1.html, (26 May 2001)

"Juanita Broaddrick: Dan Rather's Comments 'Sickened Me,'" *NewsMax*, 20 May 2001, [Online] Available http://www.news max.com/showinside.shtml?a=2001/5/20/141144, (19 June 2001)

"Judicial Watch, Inc. vs. United States Department of Commerce," *Judicial Watch*, [Online] Available http://procatalog.com/judicialWatch/cases/2/112.asp, (10 June 2001)

"Judicial Watch-Clinton Lawyer Admits Willey Documents Released to Influence Lewinsky Investigation," *Reagan Information Interchange*, 13 June 2000, [Online] Available http://reagan.com/HotTopics.main/HotMike/document-6.13.2000.5.html, (18 May 2001)

"Judicial Watch-Defense Secretary Implicated in Violation of Linda Tripp's Privacy Rights," *Reagan Information Interchange*, 25 May 2000, [Online] Available http://reagan.com/HotTopics.main/HotMike/document-5.26.2000.6.html, (9 May 2001)

"Ken Starr Gets His Day; Media Had All Year," *Media Reality Check*, 18 November 1998, [Online] Available http://www.media research.org/news/reality/1998/fax19981118.html, (28 June 2001)

King, John, and Bob Franken, and Matt Smith, "Clinton admits misleading testimony avoids charges in Lewinsky probe," *CNN All Politics*, 19 January 2001, [Online] Available http://fyi.cnn.com/2001/ALLPOLITICS/stories/01/19/clinton.lewinsky/, (28 March 2001)

Kondracke, Morton, "GOP must launch new probe of Chinagate," *Jewish World Review*, 9 August 1999, [Online] Available http://www.jewishworld.com/cols/kondracke080999.asp, (16 June 2001)

Kurtz, Howard, "Starr is Urged to Curtail Inquiry," *Washington Post*, 2 March 1998, [Online] Available http://www.washington post.com/wp-srv/politivs/special/clinton/stories/starr030298.htm, (3 May 2001)

Kurtz, Howard, "The Defenders," *Washington Post*, November 1, 1998, [Online] Available http://washingtonpost.com/wp-srv/ politics/special/clinton/stories/kurtz1101198full.htm, (24 April 2001)

Labaton, Stephen, "A Clinton Friend Admits Mail Fraud and Tax Evasion," *New York Times*, 7 December 1994, [Online] Available http://www.nytimes.com/books/97/12/14/home/12079hubbell.html, (22 May 2001)

LaFraniere, Sharon, "Clinton Told of Cash Raised From Coffees," *Washington Post*, 23 March 1997, [Online] Available http://washingtonpost.com/wp-srv/politics/special/campfin/coffees/ fundraising.htm, (26 February 2001)

"L.D. Brown Testifies About White House Intimidation," *Washington Weekly*, 6 October 1997, [Online] Available http:// www.idfiles.com/ld-brown-testifies.htm, (8 March 2001)

Leen, Jeff, "Defense Department Probes Report of Linda Tripp Arrest," *Washington Post*, 14 March 1998, http:// www.washingtonpost.com/wp-srv/politics/special/clinton/stories/ tripp031498.htm, (9 May 2001)

Levin, Mark, "The Clinton Clan," *National Review*, 22 February 2001, [Online] Available http://www.nationalreview.com/contributors/levin022201.shtml, (3 June 2001)

Levin, Mark, "The Failed Political Prosecution," *National Review*, 24 May 2000, http://www.nationalreview.com/comment/comment052400c.html, (11 June 2001)

"The Lies of Hillary Clinton," [Online] Available http://www.wickedwitch.org/lies/lies3.htm, (25 March 2001)

Limbacher, "Clinton-Connected Bribes, Break-ins, Beatings, Death Threats," 12 October 1998, [Online] Available http://www.daywilliams.com.clinton_intimidation.html, (15 May 2001)

"Lincoln Bedroom Guests Gave DNC At Least $5.2 Million," *CNN All Politics*, 1997, [Online] Available http://www.cnn.com/ALLPOLITICS/1997/02/25/lincoln.donors/index.html, (26 February 2001)

"Linda Tripp Suing Pentagon over leaks designed to 'sabotage' career," *CNN*, 25 January 2001, [Online] Available http://www.cnn.com/2001/LAW/01/25/tripp.lawsuit.02/, (9 May 2001)

"Lippo Scandal Unfolds The White House Indonesia Connection," *Washington Weekly*, 21 October 1998, [Online] Available http://www.washington-weekly.com/oct21-96/Lippo, (8 February 2001)

Locy, Toni, "Ex-Housing Chief Cisneros Indicted," *Washington Post*, 12 December 1997, [Online] Available http://cgi1.washingtonpost.com/wp-srv/politics/special/cisneros/stories/cis121297.htm, (22 May 2001)

"Majority Report: Executive Summary," *Washington Post*, 5 March 1998, [Online] Available http://washingtonpost.com/wp-srv/politics/special/campfin/stories/execsumm030698.htm, (26 February 2001)

Marcus, Ruth, "Constitutional Clash Evokes Watergate Era," *Washington Post*, 6 May 1998, [Online] Available http://www.washingtonpost.com/wp-srv/politics/special/clinton/stories/legal050698.htm, (8 April 2001)

McDonald, Marci, "A Gore moneyman at sex scandal's center," *U.S. News*, 30 March 1998, [Online] Available http://www.usnews.com/usnews/issues/980330/30land.htm, (9 March 2001)

"Michael Brown Sentenced to Minor Violation of Campaign Finance law in Face of Evidence That He Was Conduit of Bribes to His Father, Former Clinton Cabinet Secretary Ron Brown," *Judicial Watch*, 21 November 1997, [Online] Available http://www.judicialwatch.org/1997/112197a.htm, (9 June 2001)

Miller, Bill, "Cisneros Pleads Guilty to Lying to FBI Agents," *Washington Post*, 8 September 1999, [Online] Available http://cgi1.washingtonpost.com/wp-srv/politics/special/cisneros/stories/cisneros090899.htm

Mitchell, Paul, "Welcome to the Club!," 5 December 2000, [Online] Available http://www.flash.net/~pmitchel/dec52000.htm, (3 May 2000)

Molchan, Andrew, "'Trailer Park trash'," 20 March 1998, [Online] Available http://www.amfire.com/mar20.htm, (19 May 2001)

Momenteller, Bob, "Big Mouth Carville's Last Stand," *Ether Zone*, 1 July 1998, [Online] Available http://etherzone.com/carville.html, (3 May 2001)

"More Justice Department Antics," *Judicial Watch*, 24 April 2000, [Online] Available http://www.judicialwatch.org/press_release.asp?pr_id=378, (13 June 2001)

Morris, Dick, "Jim Guy's Hush Money," [Online] Available http://www.zoshow.com/News/Newsbytes/tidbits31.htm, (1 June 2001)

Morrison, Micah "Who is Dan Lasater?," *Wall Street Journal*, 7 August 1995

Mostert, Mary, "What WAS the "Message" Sent to Kathleen Willey via Car Vandalism, and an Executed Cat?," *Reagan Information Interchange*, 18 June 1998, [Online] Available http://reagan.com/HotTopics.main/HotMike/document-6.19.1998.9.html, (18 May 2001)

Mostert, Mary, "George W Bush, When Did you Stop Beating Your Wife?," *Reagan Information Interchange*, 19 August 1999, [Online] Available http://reagan.com/HotTopics.main/HotMike/documents-8.19.1999.8.html, (28 May 2001)

Murtha, Joseph, "Statement of Joseph Murtha Lead Criminal Defense Attorney For Linda R. Tripp," *FreeRepublic*, 24 May 2000, [Online] Available http://www.freerepublic.com/forum/a392c509c6467.htm, (11 June 2001)

"Networks Continue to Ignore news Broken by Newspapers on ChinaGate," *Media Research Center*, 26 June 1998, [Online] Available http://www.mediaresearch.org/press/news/pr19980626.html, (20 June 2001)

"New Evidence Links White House to Effort to Destroy Linda Tripp," *Judicial Watch*, 5 October 1999, http://www.judicial watch.org/press_release.asp?pr_id=204, (9 May 2001)

"New White House Whistle Blower Claims Intimidation," 8 November 2000, [Online} Available http://www.warroom.com/ Latest%20News/whistleblower.htm, (14 February 2001)

New York Times editorial, "Mrs. Clinton's Book Deal," *New York Times*, 22 December 2000, [Online} Available http://lists.essential. org/pipermail/cong-reform/2000/000008.html, (7 April 2001)

"NewsBites," *Media Research Center*, 22 February 1999, [Online} Available http://www.mediaresearch.org/news/mediawatch/ 1999/mw19990222nbites.html, (21 June 2001)

NewsMax staff, "Burton Tells Reno to Clear Her Skirts," *FreeRepublic*, 29 March 2000, [Online} Available http:// www.freerepublic.com/forum/a38e1cf90471d.htm, (13 June 2001)

"Nolanda Hill on Her Relationship With Ron Brown," *ABC News*, 30 July 1999, [Online} Available http://www.whatreally happened.com/RANCHO/CRASH/BROWN/nolanda.html, (29 May 2001)

Nordlinger, Jay, "Why Didn't Bacon Get Fried?," *Weekly Standard*, 12 June 2000, [Online} Available http://www.frontpage mag.com/frontlines/june00/ws06-06-00.html, (9 May 2001)

Novak, Robert, "'Filegate' ready to swing open," 8 July 1999, http://www.usclu.org/articles/filegate.html, (12 April 2001)

O'Connor, Eileen, "Clinton Allies Attack Starr Again," *CNN All Politics*, 1 March 1998, [Online} Available http://www.cnn.com/ ALLPOLITICS/1998/03/01/clinton.lewinsky/, (3 May 2001)

Olson, Theodore, "The Most Political Justice Department Ever: A Survey," *American Spectator*, 11 September 2000, [Online] Available http://www.spectator.org/archives/0009TAS/olson0009.htm, (12 June 2001)

"Opening Statement by Representative Bill McCollum at Impeachment of William J. Clinton," 15 January 1999, [Online] Available http://wwww.senate.gov/~rpc/archive/impeach/mccollum 1-15.htm, (February 5 2001)

"Pentagon investigating whether Tripp lied about her background," 15 March 1998, [Online] Available http://capitol hillblue.com/March1998/trippmar15.htm, (9 May 2001)

"Petition for Order to Show Cause Why William Jefferson Clinton Should Not Be Held in Criminal Contempt of Court," *Judicial Watch*, [Online] Available http://www.judicialwatch.org/archive/ois/cases/browning/DKBcontPet.htm, (12 May 2001)

Powers, William, "Media Rex: Scandal-Shy," *New Republic*, 16 December 1996, [Online] Available http://thenewrepublic.com/archive/1996/12/121696/powers121696.html, (21 June 2001)

Rabinowitz, Dorothy, "Wall Street Journal Editorial Commentary-Juanita Broaddrick Meets the Press," *Wall Street Journal*, 19 February 1999, [Online] Available http://www.shamema.com/wsjbroad.htm, (16 February 2001)

"Recovered history-What various people said when Newt Gingrich got $4.5 million in book deal," *FreeRepublic*, 19 December 2000, [Online] Available http://www.freerepublic.com/foruma 3a3fd28312b3.htm, (7 April 2001)

Regnery, Alfred, "Mrs. Clinton's Book Deal," 29 December 2000, *Human Events*, [Online] Available http://www.human eventsonline.com/articles/12-29-00/regnery.html, (7 April 2001)

"Reno Justice Department Retaliates Against Witness in Clinton Fundraising Scandal," *Judicial Watch*, 24 March 1998, http://www.judicialwatch.org/1998/032498.htm, (10 June 2001)

"Rep. Traficant on IRS Audits Paula Jones Who Has no Income," *Reagan Information Interchange*, 16 September 1997, [Online] Available http://reagan.com/HotTopics.main/HotMike/document-9.18.1997.6.html, (19 May 2001)

"Report: McDougal had no access to heart drug, doctors just before death," *CNN All Politics*, 14 September 1998, [Online] Available http://www.cnn.com/ALLPOLITICS/stories/1998/09/14/mcdougal/, (25 May 2001)

"Rose law firm billing records," *PBS Frontline*, 1998, [Online] Available http://www.pbs.org/wgbh/pages/frontline/shows/arkansas/docs/recs.html, (9 February 2001)

Safire, William, "The 100,000 E-Mail Gap," *FreeRepublic*, 29 March 2000, [Online] Available http://www.freerepublic.com/foruma38e2e3b7591d.htm, (14 February 2001)

Schmidt, Susan, and Peter Baker, "McDougal Indicted for Silence on Whitewater," *Washington Post*, 5 May 1998, [Online] Available http://www.washingtonpost.com/wp-srv/politics/special/clinton/stories/starr050598.htm, (25 May 2001)

Schmidt, Susan, "J. McDougal Book Says Clinton Lied Under Oath," *Washington Post*, 19 May 1998, [Online] Available http://www.washingtonpost.com/wp-srv/politics/special/clinton/stories/mcdougal051998.htm, (3 June 2001)

Schmidt, Susan, "Hubbell Got $700,000 for Little or No Work, House Probe Says," *Washington Post*, [Online} Available http://www.washingtonpost.com/wp-srv/politics/special/clinton/stories/hubbell042498.htm, (31 May 2001)

Schmidt, Susan, "Starr Probing Willey Allegations," *Washington Post*, 1 November 1998, [Online} Available http://www.washingtonpost.com/wp-srv/politics/special/clinton/stories/willey110198.htm, (18 May 2001)

Schmidt, Susan, "Tyson Foods Admits Illegal Gifts to Espy," *Washington Post*, 30 December 1997, [Online} Available http://www.washingtonpost.com/wp-srv/politics/special/counsels/stories/espy123097.htm, (28 May 2001)

Shannan, Pat, "'Failure of Public Trust'," *Media Bypass*, 27 April 2001, [Online} Available http://www.4bypass.com/archives/may-00.htm, (15 May 2001)

Snow, Tony, "Tripp: 'Fear is a magnificent motivator'," 1998, *Detroit News*, [Online} Available http://detnews.com/VOICES/SNOW/980803/980803.htm, (9 May 2001)

Sohn, Emily, "The young and the virtueless," *U.S. News & World Report*, 21 May 2001, 51

"The Special Committee's Whitewater Report," [Online} Available http://www.whatreallyhappened.com/RANCHO/POLITICS/WW/white6.html, (5 February 2001)

Sperry, Paul, "CNN, ABC spike reports after taping interviews with e-mail whistle blower," *FreeRepublic*, 29 March 2001, [Online} Available http://www.freerepublic.com/forum/a38e1cf90471d.htm, (14 February 2001)

Sperry, Paul, "All the President's Scandals," *FreeRepublic*, 29 March 2001, [Online} Available http://www.freerepublic.com/forum/a38e1cf90471d.htm, (14 February 2001)

"The Starr Report," *Washington Post*, 9 September 1998, [Online} Available http://www.washingtonpost.com/wp-srv/politics/special/clinton/stories/6narritxiv.htm, http://www.washingtonpost.com/wp-srv/politics/special/clinton/stories/7groundsvii.htm, http://www.washingtonpost.com/wp-srv/politics/special/clinton/stories/6narritxi.htm, http://www.washingtonpost.com/wp-srv/politics/special/clinton/stories/6narritxiii.htm, (5 February 2001)

"The Stats," *Media Research Center*, 8 January 1998, [Online] Available www.mediaresearch.org/specialreports/news/tcstat.html, (5 August 2001)

Stephanopoulos, George, <u>All Too Human</u>, United States, Little, Brown And Company, 1999

Straub, Bill, "What now for Paula Jones?," *Nando*, 1998, [Online} Available http://archive.nando times.com/newsroom/nt/402paula0.html, (19 May 2001)

Suro, Roberto, and Toni Locy, "Indictment Secured In Fund Probe," *Washington Post*, 29 January 1998, [Online} Available http://www.washingtonpost.com/wp-srv/politics/special/campfin/stories/cf012998.htm, (25 May 2001)

Suro, Roberto, "U.S. Advised Starr of probe Last Month," *Washington Post*, 11 February 1999, [Online} Available http://www.washingtonpost.com/wp-srv/politics/special/clinton/stories/starr021199.htm, (11 June 2001)

"Tapes: Hubbell Showed Concern About First Lady's Legal Work," *CNN All Politics*, 1 May 1998, [Online} Available http://www.cnn.com/ALLPOLITICS/1998/05/01/hubbell/, (31 May 2001)

"Terry McAuliffe DNC National Chair," [Online} Available http://www.democrats.org/hq/leadership/bios/mcauliffe.html, (24 May 2001)

"Time For Him to Go," *New Republic*, 8 March 2001, [Online} Available http://www.thenewrepublic.com/031901/editorial 031901.html, (24 May 2001)

"TV's Top Ten Undercovered Stories," *MediaWatch*, January 1997, [Online} Available http://www.mediaresearch.org/news/mediawatch/1997/mw19970101stud.html, (28 June 2001)

Tumulty, Karen, "The Hubbell Rescue Mission," *CNN All Politics*, 14 April 1997, [Online} Available http://www.cnn.com/ALLPOLITICS/1997/04/07/time/hubbell.html, (31 May 2001)

"Update on Linda Tripp File Case," *Reagan Information Interchange*, 10 May 2000, [Online} Available http://reagan.com/HotTopics.main/HotMike/document-5.10.2000.3.html, (9 May 2001)

"U.S. National Security and Military/Commercial Concerns with the People's Republic of China," 3 January 1999, [Online} Available http://hillsource.house.gov/CoxReport/body/ch9bod.html, (8 February 2001).

Van Natta, Don, "Drug Smuggler Made Clinton Donation in Cuba, Investigators say," *New York Times*, 2000, [Online} Available http://www.lanuevacuba.com/archivo/cabrera03.htm, (24 May 2001)

Wall Street Journal editorial, "'Don't You Get the Message?' ," *Wall Street Journal*, 26 October 1998

Wall Street Journal editorial, "The Livingstone Standard," *Wall Street Journal*, 28 June 1996, A8

Wall Street Journal editorial, "The New Senate Politics," *Wall Street Journal*, 5 June 2001, A26

Wall Street Journal editorial, "Obstruction of Justice Department," *Wall Street Journal*, 30 September 1999

Wall Street Journal editorial, "The Sixth Month Gap," *Wall Street Journal*, 14 October 1996

"The Washington Times-Ex-Trooper Will Tell of Bribery Attempt," *Reagan Information Interchange*, 25 August 1997, [Online} Available http://www.reagan.com/HotTopics.main/ HotMike/document-8.25.1997.6html, (5 February 2001)

Werner, Erica, "Won't Retry McDougal on contempt counts, Starr says," *Arkansas Democrat-Gazette*, 26 May 1999, [Online] Available http://www.ardemgaz.com/prev/clinton/acxstarr 052699.html, (25 May 2001)

Whitcomb, Dan, "Clinton Friend Riady Pleads Guilty, Fined S8.6 Million," *FreeRepublic*, 20 March 2001, [Online} Available http:// www.freerepublic.com/forum/a3ab720344c29.htm, (27 May 2001)

"White House Threatens Contractors with Jail," [Online} Available http://www.pipebombnews.com/index.cfm?page= contractors.htm, (14 February 2001)

"Who Said Linda Tripp had Rights?," *MediaWatch*, 5 October 1998, [Online} Available http://www.mediaresearch.org/news/ mediawatch/1998/mw19981005rev.html, (27 June 2001)

"Why the Difference?," *Times & Free Press*, 14 March 1999, [Online} Available http://www.timesfreepress.com/opinion/fpedit/1999/Mar/Mar141999fpedit3.html, (18 June 2001)

"The Wild Swings in Hubbell's Relevance," *Media* Watch, 8 February 1999, [Online} Available http://www.media research.org/news/mediawatch/1999/mw19990208p1.html, (28 June 2001)

"Willey Law Suit," [Online} Available http://209.235.49.36/media/preleases/willey.htm, (18 May 2001)

"The Willey letters," *Washington Post*, 16 March 1998, [Online} Available http://www.washingtonpost.com/wp-srv/politics/special/clinton/stories/willeyletters.htm, [18 May 2001]

Woodman, Sue, "Are You Prepared For Puberty?," *Family Life*, June/July 2001, 60-64

York, Byron, "Carville's Cast of Characters," *American Spectator*, August 1997, [Online} Available http://www.spectator.org/archives97-08_york.html, (3 May 2000)

York, Byron, "Michael Brown Goes Free," *American Spectator*, November 1997, [Online} Available http://www.spectator.org/archives/97-11_york.html, (9 June 2001)

Yost, Pete, "President denies Willey accusations," *Nando Times*, 1998, [Online} Available http://www.nando.net/nt/special/fredmize0316.html, (9 March 2001)

"You've Lost Mail: The White House Email Saga," *Harvard Law*, 3 May 2000, [Online} Available http://cyber.law.harvard.edu/digitaldiscovery/digdisc_library_6.html, (14 February 2001)

Young, Rick, "The Castle Grande Deal," *PBS Frontline*, 1998, [Online] Available http://www.pbs.org/wgbh/pages/frontline/shows/arkansas/castle/ (9 February 2001)

Zeifman, Jerome, "Zeifman Memo to Rep. Barr on Clinton Impeachment," *Chuck Baldwin Live*, 18 November 1998, [Online] Available http://www.chuckbaldwinlive.com/read.bribery.html, (5 March 2001)

GI